Workbook

for

Levin and Fox

Elementary Statistics in Social Research
The Essentials

Second Edition

prepared by

David R. Forde
University of Memphis

PEARSON

Boston   New York   San Francisco
Mexico City   Montreal   Toronto   London   Madrid   Munich   Paris
Hong Kong   Singapore   Tokyo   Cape Town   Sydney

ISBN 13: 978-0-205-51683-4
ISBN 10: 0-205-51683-1

Printed in the United States of America

10 9 8 7 6 5 4 3 2 1   10 09 08 07 06

TABLE OF CONTENTS

PREFACE

This workbook includes a series of exercises that is designed to complement topics covered in Levin and Fox's *Elementary Statistics in Social Research: The Essentials*, 2nd Edition. Their textbook emphasizes theoretical issues, shows how to complete hand computation of statistics, and demonstrates applications of statistics. This workbook emphasizes using a computer to obtain the information and the "interpretation" and "presentation" of results of statistical analysis.

The material in the workbook includes:
- Computer lab activities with problems and solutions in each chapter
- Basic computer commands for the Statistical Package for the Social Sciences (SPSS © Student Version 12.0 and 13.0 and Full Version 14.0)
- Instructional codebooks
- Instructions for using James Alan Fox's *Statistics Calculator*
- A brief discussion of research articles
- Exercises and work-sheets in each chapter

Additional materials and software for the exercises in this workbook requires:
- Access to SPSS software. SPSS software is available as 1) full version, 2) graduate package, 3) SPSS career starter, and 4) student version. For the full version, many Universities and Colleges provide access to site-licensed use of SPSS (full version) in their computer labs. Some students may wish to purchase the graduate package or career starter versions which include the base and advanced statistics, regression, and AMOS software with no limits on variables or cases. Other students wishing to work on their own computers may purchase SPSS student version which allows users to work with smaller datasets (50 variables and 1500 cases). The SPSS student packages have a four year license for student home use.
- Obtaining a copy of the instructional data sets from the web-site (see information about downloading on page iii of this preface);
- Microsoft Excel© in order to use Fox's *Statistics Calculator*

STATISTICS IN SOCIAL SCIENCES

Working with statistics in the social sciences can be both interesting and informative. I'd like to ask you a few questions before we start:

1. How many murders were there last year in the United States?   (Your answer)_____

2. How many close friends do you have that you can confide in, and how many close friends does an average American have as a close confidant?
(Your answers) _____; _____

For some reason, most Americans fear numbers. John Allen Paulos (1990) in *Innumeracy: Mathematical Illiteracy and Its Consequences* wrote about how most people will not tolerate illiteracy yet they will neglect to learn about numbers making incredible bungles. Vandiver and Giacopassi (1997) report that most students don't have a good grasp of crime numbers as they greatly overestimate the extent of crime. Compare your guesses on murder and friends to the information that follows.

In 2004, there were about 16,137 murders (including non-negligent manslaughter) which is about 5.5 murders per 100,000 persons in the United States. You can obtain yearly estimates on homicide from the Federal Bureau of Investigation in their annual report on *Crime in the United States: Uniform Crime Reports*. It is also available on-line at www.fbi.gov in the link to "publications."

Using information from the 2004 General Social Survey (GSS), McPherson, Smith-Lovin and Brashears (2006) estimate that Americans have 2.08 confidants with whom they can discuss important matters. The results of their article can be read in the June 2006 issue of the *American Sociological Review*.

How close were your guesses?   What factors might explain why some people make guesses that are far away from the actual numbers? Are these "official" statistics about homicide provided by governmental agencies even accurate? Can the GSS where a few thousand people were asked questions really help us to understand social trends in the whole of the United States? Wow! These are hard questions to answer.

If we as a society really want to tackle social problems such as crime, poverty, racial inequality, and other issues, we are going to need to work to obtain a basic grasp of statistics. My challenge to you is to go through the exercises in this book thinking about how the numbers work and how you can best present the information so that a non-statistician will understand what you have done.

Let's go get the data files and get started with these exercises.

WEB-SITE FOR DATASETS

The instructional SPSS datasets are located on the Allyn and Bacon Web-site as a supplement to Levin and Fox's textbook. You will need to have internet access using a browser such as Internet Explorer. Type the link address into the address line in the browser as:

`http://ablongman.com/levinfox/`

Additional instructions will be provided on the web-page, but the basics are:

- Get a jump drive (portable drive / memory stick, or a diskette)
- Go to the web-site and click on the links to save the SPSS files to the device where you wish to store the data

There are two SPSS files to download:

- MTF 2004.sav – A subset of variables from the 2004 Monitoring the Future Study

- GSS 2004.sav – A subset of variables from the 2004 General Social Survey

JAMES ALAN FOX'S STATISTICS CALCULATOR

James Alan Fox has developed a statistics calculator for textbooks that he has written with Jack Levin and published with Allyn and Bacon. The Allyn and Bacon calculator – ABCalc – is available as a file for download from the web-site for this textbook.

You must have Microsoft Excel© to use this calculator. The file is quite large at about 5.6 MB. I recommend that you download it on to a portable drive. Once you have the file and you are working on a computer that has Excel, click on the file to start the calculator. The main menu is shown below.

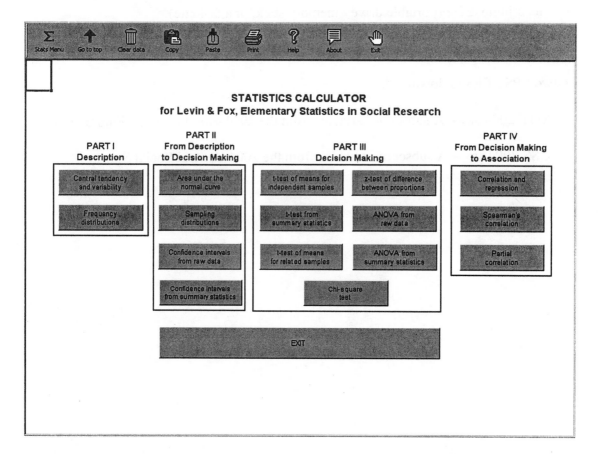

This statistics calculator is very easy to use. It calculates statistics as you enter data into a spreadsheet. You will see examples of how to use it in later chapters. It is an excellent tool for small data sets where you are entering the data directly into the program.

A short manual for ABCalc is also available from the web-site. This lab manual also has most basic instructions for the calculator.

RESEARCH ARTICLES

Whether you are writing a paper that is reviewing literature or writing about your own research project, it is important that you are able to find research articles, to understand them, to summarize their findings, and that you compare them to your own research. Keep track of where you find things. Accurate and complete citations are important for documenting the source of information. A research methods class will focus on how the information was sampled. In this workbook, we will focus on how to develop an effective summary of statistical information.

College and university libraries have collections of leading scholarly and peer-reviewed journals in Sociology, Psychology, Criminal Justice, and many more areas. Many libraries have on-line research tools that allow students to use keywords to search for articles. As you develop your research skills, you should begin to familiarize yourself with downloading of abstracts, reading of full text of articles, e-mailing of searches, and downloading of Adobe Acrobat files (original format).

Keep in mind that Internet based searches are not usually an acceptable method of doing a research paper because most journal searches are not freely available on the Internet. As a social researcher, you should learn how to access on-line periodical search engines in your college or university library system (e.g. Sociofile, PsychLit, etc.) and paper abstracting sources such as Sociological Abstracts or Psychological Abstracts.

Keywords and phrases can be used in electronic searches. While you can type in any work into a search engine, you should have a look at the "thesaurus" of key words to see the kinds of words that are used to catalog articles. If you look at the details within a search you may also see the specific keywords that were used when an article was archived. These library data bases are updated regularly.

As you do library searches, you may wish to add additional terms to focus upon a more specific issue when you find a very large number of articles for your topic. It is a good idea to read the abstracts to learn more about an article. The abstract will help you to determine whether the article is directly related to the topic that you want to study. If they're not, you may need to narrow or expand your search terms.

When I do searches I e-mail the results of the search to my own account. An e-mail of abstracts and sources will help you to document your search and to keep an accurate list of references for your research.

Additional Readings

American Psychological Association (2001). *Publication Manual of the American Psychological Association.* Washington, DC: APA

> The APA manual is used by many social science journals as a referencing tool. It provides guidelines on organizing papers, presenting statistical information, and citation of references.

Huff, D.H. (1993). *How to Lie with Statistics.* W.W. Norton and Company.

> This classic is a small book first published in 1954. Huff shows how numbers can be used to oversimplify, bamboozle, confuse, and terrorize the general public. I strongly recommend it.

Paulos, J.A. (1990). *Innumeracy: Mathematical Illiteracy and Its Consequences.* Vintage Books.

> Paulos coins the term innumeracy as analogous to illiteracy.

McPherson, M., Smith-Lovin, L., & Brashears, M.E. (2006). Social Isolation in America: Changes in Core Discussion Networks Over Two Decades. *American Sociological Review, 71,* 353-75.

> McPherson and associates discuss how American's close confidants have declined over time. They discuss reasons for this decline and suggest that this is an important social change in America.

Vandiver, M., & Giacopassi, D. (1997). One Million and Counting: Students' Estimates of the Annual Number of Homicides in the U.S. *Journal of Criminal Justice Education,* 8, 135-143.

> Vandiver and Giacopassi report how students overestimate the murder rate and they discuss some reasons why this may happen.

Acknowledgements

I would like to thank the Principal Investigators of the Monitoring the Future Study and Dr. Tom Smith of the General Social Survey for permitting me to use their data sets. Thanks also to my wife Linda for her support, to the many students who've used earlier versions of this workbook, to James Fox for his comments, and to Lance Roberts and Mike Gillespie who "bothered me" a whole lot when I had to learn statistics. Any errors in this workbook though are mine.

STATISTICAL ANALYSIS: READY OR NOT, LET'S GO!

INTRODUCTION

Chapter1A is designed to ease you into analyzing data sets by introducing the Statistical Package for Social Sciences (SPSS ©), codebooks, and some descriptive statistics. These data sets will be analyzed using SPSS Version 14.0 for Windows. It assumes that you have obtained the instructional datasets. If you have not, please read the web-site section in the preface to this workbook.

In this chapter you will see that statistical analysis looks complex on a first attempt, but that it is quite easy to complete if you proceed systematically, identify basic assumptions about variables, choose a statistical procedure, generate the computer output, and then interpret it. Just keep in mind that you will be building a repertoire of analytic skills as you complete each chapter.

CODEBOOKS

The data sets used in these exercises are drawn from publicly available data library files of the Inter-university Consortium for Political and Social Research (ICPSR). Two different studies are used:
1. The Monitoring the Future Study, 2004 (Appendix A);
2. The General Social Survey, 2004 (Appendix B).

You will need to read the codebooks to learn the format and placement of the data. Read the preface and introduction of each codebook for a brief explanation of these data. We will use a small subset of questions excerpted from each of these studies. These data sets and questions from each were selected because they cover a broad range of issues in the social sciences.

Codebooks are important because they tell us about the kinds of information that are stored in a data set. We will want to know about variables and their attributes. In order to do this using SPSS, we will need to know a variable's acronym, and how its attributes are coded. Different researchers may use different methods of coding information and you, as a researcher, will need to read the codebook in order to understand how a data set is put together.

Let's start by looking at the codebook from the Monitoring the Future Study. Flip to Appendix A. You'll see a brief description of when and how the data set was collected. Notice that this codebook is a small subset of questions taken from the larger study. It also uses only a random sample of 1500 cases from the original study. The information in this codebook is extracted so that we can see the exact wording of questions and whether a question is part of a larger section. We are going to want to identify the following:

- Variable acronyms (or mneumonics)

- Variable labels
- Value labels (Coding categories)
- Missing values

Figure 1 highlights the key components of the variable identified as V104 which examines alcohol consumption. The researchers who made the codebook for the Monitoring the Future Study have numbered questions as the letter "V" followed by a number. Notice also that the questions on the survey are notated as "B" 04, 04a, et cetera. The Monitoring the Future Study is extremely large and cross references will help you to locate variables and questions if you wish to use the larger study or you are reading a publication from it.

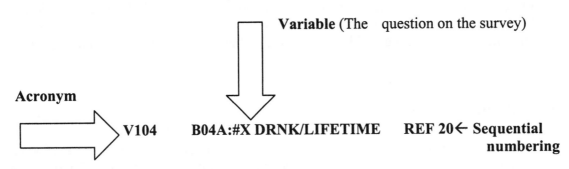

Variable (The   question on the survey)

Acronym

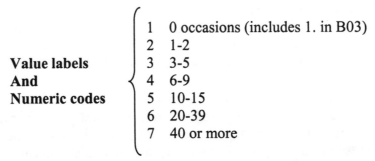

V104   **B04A:#X DRNK/LIFETIME**   **REF 20**← Sequential
                                                             numbering

               MISSING -9

B04: On how many occasions have you had alcoholic beverages to drink...

B04a: Alcohol in your lifetime?

	1	0 occasions (includes 1. in B03)
	2	1-2
Value labels	3	3-5
And	4	6-9
Numeric codes	5	10-15
	6	20-39
	7	40 or more

Figure 1 Breaking down the key components of a variable in a codebook

Looking at Figure 1, the variable acronym for this question is V104. It is important to know this fact because "V104" is used to identify the variable in the SPSS file. Take a moment to identify other variable acronyms in the codebook. I have also added a reference number to each variable in this codebook to provide a sequential location of the variables. V104 is the 20th variable in the dataset for this workbook. Soon you will see that SPSS can locate a variable based on an alphabetical listing of acronyms or by their sequential ordering within the data file.

This variable "V104" represents information about students' lifetime consumption of alcoholic beverages. This codebook provides the exact wording of the question and how responses were recorded for each variable. In most instances, this codebook it is quite clear in identifying the topic of study. In the future, as you read other codebooks, you will see that the Monitoring the Future Study is an example of a "very good" codebook. Looking now at Figure 2, note that the variable V104 is labeled by these researchers as "042B04A #X ALC LIF SIPS."

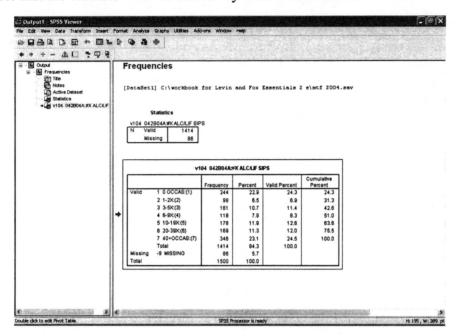

Figure 2 SPSS Output showing the frequency distribution for variable V104

A good variable label should be descriptive. You will see several instances in the Monitoring the Future Study (MTF) where you will have to go to its codebook in order to decipher the question that was asked. While the MTF is a fabulous study, the researchers have used many abbreviations which are not intuitive and sometimes are indecipherable (at least, to my weak eyes). It is a good practice to try to make labels that describe the variable, and to always go back to the codebook to ensure that you have a clear understanding of what the variable is designed to measure.

Next, let's go back to Figure 1 and say that you were asked to find out how many students had never had a drink of alcohol in their lifetime. Here the coding category for your answer is the numeric code of "1." Looking at the valid percentages, I see that about 24 percent of high school students in 2004 said that they had never had an alcoholic beverage in their lifetime.

A final part in reading a question in a codebook is "missing values." In the Monitoring the Future Codebook, the missing values are stated immediately below each question as the number or numbers that will be excluded (-9 for V104). Sometimes codebooks will denote missing values by placing the letter "**M**" beside values that will be excluded in statistical analysis. When doing our analysis, we would like to know how many people answer the question (valid responses) and how many people did not answer it (missing responses). Look at Figure 2 now and you'll see that information that is missing is reported at the bottom of the frequency table. There were 86 students (5.7 percent) who did not answer this question.

Learning to read a codebook is an important part of data analysis. You will need to know where variables are located in a dataset, how things are labeled, and whether there are any missing values for a variable. Note also that this codebook presents the questions on the survey in the order that the questions were asked. Another codebook may present questions in alphanumeric sequence (A's, B's, C's, etc.; or as var1, var2, var3, etc.). It is very important to read the codebook to learn how the data set was put together.

LEVELS OF MEASUREMENT

Variables may be characterized on many dimensions. It is important to understand the properties of variables because the types of analysis a researcher may do depends on how a variable is measured and treated. This workbook provides a brief introduction to four traditional levels of measurement: nominal, ordinal, interval, and ratio.

Levels of measurement

Level	Properties				Codebook
Nominal	difference				V13
Ordinal	difference	rank			V163
Interval	difference	rank	equidistant		V1643
Ratio	difference	rank	equidistant	zero	V197

Nominal measures simply imply a difference in categories of a variable. While a number is assigned to each category there is no inherent meaning beyond a difference in the categories. Examples of nominal measurement include sex and race. Sex is a variable with two categories (dichotomous): male and female. Region, in this dataset, is a variable with four categories: Northeast, North Central, South, and West. The numbers assigned to each category are referred to as codes rather than values since they (the numbers) have no meaning. For example, in coding region, each category is coded as a number from 1 to 4 but no order is implied in assigning a number.

Ordinal measures classify a difference and rank order categories. They do not tell us how much of a difference there is between cases or the difference between a case and a real zero. They simply compare a category with other categories (or a set of categories) of a variable. They do not have a standardized metric.

Interval measures classify differences, rank, and imply equidistance between categories. Interval measures rely on a metric or standard unit of measurement. These are sometimes called scales or scalar measures.

Ratio measures are the highest level. They have all of the properties of each of the other types of variables: differences, rank, equidistance between values of categories, plus a real zero. For example, age in years can be considered as a ratio variable with zero being birth and each unit representing one year of time. Note that Levin and Fox combined ratio with interval measures. In practice, the same statistic is used for both interval and ratio level variables.

It is important that you, as a researcher, are able to recognize the properties of variables. In each of the labs you will be asked to consider the level of measurement and whether a metric is **discrete** or **continuous**. These decisions will influence how you may interpret statistical analysis of a metric. For example, in interpreting age as a continuous variable you would then assume that values between integers are valid (e.g 13.4 years is a valid possibility between 13 and 14). Lastly, you must consider whether the variable is treated as **dependent** or **independent**. Treatment of variables as dependent or independent will allow you to examine one or more variables as the cause of another which is a theoretical issue, not a statistical issue. For example, sex, race, and family characteristics are variables that generally are treated as independent variables while others are examined as dependent variables.

Note, while you will be asked to identify each of the levels of measurement, you should also be aware that ordinal variables are the most difficult to work with statistically. There are two methods to get around problems with ordinal variables. First, one can treat an ordinal variable as if it is nominal and proceed with nominal level statistics; or, second, more commonly one can treat the categories as if they are interval assuming that values represent a common metric. There are advanced statistics to test the validity of an ordinal to interval assumption, but they are rarely tested. As "statisticians" we are going to want to work with statistics that will help us to best understand the relationship between variables. In some chapters, we will need to disclose our "assumptions" about using an ordinal level as an interval level measure because interval level variables allow greater flexibility in analysis than others.

GET THE DATA FILE USING SPSS

There are several ways to retrieve a data file in SPSS. A dialogue box , shown below, comes up when SPSS is started. By default, it asks whether you wish to "Open an existing data source." We're going to open an existing data file. Click on OK at the bottom of the screen.

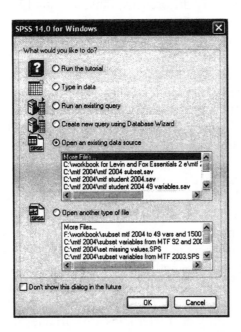

On the next screen, change the "Look in" location to where you have downloaded and stored the datasets. In this case, I am using a portable traveldrive with a folder that I have called "statistics." The traveldrive is on the F: drive of my computer. SPSS by default shows SPSS system files of type (*.sav). To retrieve the datafile, double-click on the folder and then on the filename. When successful, the data file will come up as variables in the SPSS data editor. If you do not see the spss data file listed in this window, check that your diskette is inserted into the drive, check the correct drive is listed (A, B, or perhaps a zip drive D or F). You'll need to specify the correct drive for your computer.

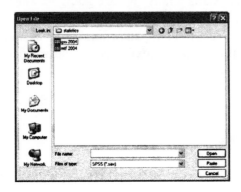

DATA ANALYSIS

The main objective of Chapter 1 is to produce a *frequency distribution* for each variable. The frequencies procedure in SPSS can be located using the drop down boxes by clicking on ANALYZE, then DESCRIPTIVE STATISTICS, and finally FREQUENCIES. The drop down box on my computer is shown below. I have set the options so that variable names (rather than labels) are shown in the order that they appear in the data file. Other people may prefer labels and alphabetical listings of acronyms.

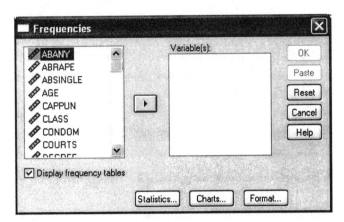

You can change these settings (and you may really want to do so!!) by clicking on EDIT and Options. You'll need to do this each time you have a session on a lab computer. You'll only need to do it once if it is on your own computer. I also have changed the output labels to "names and labels" and "values and labels." Make these changes and click apply (or close SPSS and restart it).

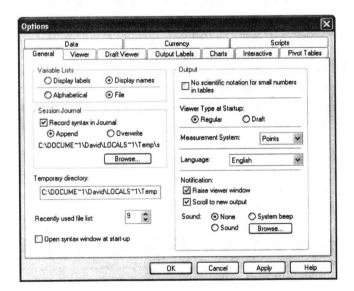

Changing the options will make it easier for you to read output and to locate variables within a data file. Try it and you'll see that it isn't too complicated. You can also proceed without making these changes.

The FREQUENCIES procedure in SPSS gives the number of times (frequency) for each value (or code) of a variable. This is reported as a proportion where the number of occurrences is divided by the total number of cases. Percentages are proportions multiplied by 100. Valid percentages are what we are most interested in where these represent the number of cases when a valid response was given.

Researchers will begin their data analysis by looking at frequencies to see the distribution of values on a variable. Is a particular value common or rare? Do people in America favor or oppose the death penalty for persons convicted of murder? You can answer this question by knowing the distribution of cases on the variable.

DATA ANALYSIS EXAMPLE

Research Problem: Are people in the United States in favor of the Death Penalty? Open the SPSS data file: **gss 2004.sav**. Find **CAPPUN** in the variable list. It is listed near the beginning of the data file. Click on Cappun and it will move to the right side of the box. Click on OK and it will generate a frequency distribution for favor or opposition to the death penalty for murder (Cappun). Provide an interpretation of the results in which you describe the variable, its level of measurement, the results of the study, and the source of your information.

Computer output: Different computer programs generate different types of output. The objective of these lab exercises is not to show you a specific type of computer output but instead to have what kinds of things you should look for in computer output. In fact, most computer programs may generate different forms of output so that the same program may provide different things for one user versus another. A sample format of computer generated output is shown for Cappun. The frequency distribution shows the variable that was analyzed, the value and label for categories, and statistical information. We are most interested in the number of valid cases, and the valid percentages. If you edit the output options, your output will look like the frequency distribution shown on the next page.

Frequencies

```
[DataSet1] F:\statistics\gss 2004.sav
```

Statistics

CAPPUN FAVOR OR OPPOSE
DEATH PENALTY FOR MURDER

N	Valid	659
	Missing	841

CAPPUN FAVOR OR OPPOSE DEATH PENALTY FOR MURDER

		Frequency	Percent	Valid Percent	Cumulative Percent
Valid	1 FAVOR	444	29.6	67.4	67.4
	2 OPPOSE	215	14.3	32.6	100.0
	Total	659	43.9	100.0	
Missing	0 NAP	790	52.7		
	8 DK	45	3.0		
	9 NA	6	.4		
	Total	841	56.1		
Total		1500	100.0		

Interpretation: Write a summary of what you've found in the computer output. Your job is to take the statistical material and to turn it into something that an educated reader may understand without having to know much (if anything) about how the analysis was done. For example, you might want to think about how you would explain your work in statistics to a friend who is not also taking this class.   A summary for this variable follows:

The General Social Survey (GSS) conducted in 2004 surveyed a random sample of Americans about a variety of social issues. The instructional data set uses a subset of 1500 cases from the GSS. The GSS included a question about whether people would favor the death penalty for persons convicted of murder. Attitudes toward capital punishment (Cappun), in this study, is measured as a nominal level variable coded as favor (1) and oppose (2). A frequency distribution shows that of persons who expressed an opinion about 67 percent of the respondents were in favor of the death penalty versus 33 percent opposed.

Notice that some respondents failed to answer this question saying they didn't know (3.0%) or refused (0.4%). A much larger percentage of people on this study are shown as "NAP" and shown as missing because they were not asked this question (52.7%). In order to shorten the time to complete a survey and to test different ways of asking questions, different people get different versions of the survey. These categories are excluded from statistical analysis using the missing values command.

There is a lot of information to include in every interpretation of statistical results. A brief checklist for a good interpretation is that it will report:

- the source of information;
- level of measurement;
- valid percentages;
- total "N" for a study;
- missing data
- and, an interesting aspect of a variable.

KEY TERMS

Acronym   Independent variable
Codebook   Missing values
Dependent variable   SPSS
Frequencies   Variable label
Levels of Measurement   Value label
     Nominal
     Ordinal
     Interval or Ratio

Name _____   Date _____

Complete the following problems.
Detach the sheets to hand them in (as requested)

CHAPTER 1 PROBLEMS

Tasks/Interpretation: Fill in the blank for each variable.

1.   You will need to become comfortable with the measurement properties of the variables. Complete the information for each variable referring to the codebook as necessary. You must determine the level of measurement for each variable. **This task can and should be completed before you go to a computer lab.**

2.   Generate a frequency distribution for each variable. Do them ONE (or a few at a time) to speed the analysis.

3.   For each variable, write a short explanation which answers the research problem (below). Your interpretation should answer the issues from the checklist (source, level of measurement, suitability of variable, valid percentages, missing data, and an interesting aspect of the data). Write your interpretations in the space that is provided.

4.   Familiarize yourself with the codebooks. You will be using them in all of the statistical exercises.

I recommend that you proceed systematically for one research problem before going on to the next one. Read the questions, use the computer, and write an interpretation before moving to the next problem.

*Research Problem*s; Use the Monitoring the Future Study, 2004 to find:

1.   What percentage of the sample is male?

2. What percentage of high school seniors has never drank alcohol? Find the variable name and the percentage for "No".

For the following variables, generate a frequency distribution and describe an aspect of the data that is of interest to you.

3. What percentage of high school students has ever smoked marijuana (or hashish)?

4. What percentage of high school students expect to graduate from a 4-year college?

5. Select a variable of interest to you. Report on an aspect of it.

Name _____   **Date** _____

Use the General Social Survey to analyze the following:

6. What percentage of Americans is afraid to walk in their own neighborhood after dark?

7. What do Americans say about their health?

8. Select a variable in the GSS of interest to you. Report on an aspect of it

9. Analyze the GSS questions on suicide: SUICIDE1, SUICIDE2, and SUICIDE4. What are the percentages of Americans that say "yes" that suicide should be allowed for persons with an incurable disease, and for each of these situations?

10. What is your opinion on these same questions about suicide?

11. What do you think may explain why some people may say yes or no to these questions?

12. Use your college library to find two articles about attitudes toward suicide. Try to identify the theories that the author(s) use to explain people's attitudes? On a separate sheet, write a two-page summary of your findings.

BUILDING A DATA FILE

INTRODUCTION

This chapter provides an introduction to the structure of data sets. It describes some of the common procedures used to create data sets using SPSS. It demonstrates how to label variables and their attributes, and discusses the importance of labeling variables and documentation of data sets. Lastly, the Inter-university Consortium for Political and Social Research (ICPSR) is introduced.

STANDARD DATA STRUCTURE

There are a wide variety of statistical analysis programs that may be used to analyze data. If you've used a computer, you may already have used a spreadsheet program such as Microsoft Excel, Microsoft Works, or Mariner Calc to balance your checkbook. These spreadsheets enable users to perform mathematical manipulations (e.g. add or subtract) down columns and across rows. Spreadsheets, however, are typically limited in the number of variables that may be included and in the ease to which statistics may be computed. People seeking to do statistical analysis more often will go to a "canned" program that is designed for computing statistics.

Two of the most readily available statistical programs are the Statistical Package for the Social Sciences (SPSS), and Statistical Analysis Systems (SAS). Both of these packages are used widely by Universities, Government, and Businesses. These programs are available for use on different kinds of computers ranging from mainframes, to local area networks, to personal computers (e.g. Windows XP).

Social scientists typically work with very large data sets. A mainframe application is used by the US Government to analyze the hundreds of variables and millions of cases in the US Census of Population. With the increased speed and power of personal computers (PC) it is now relatively easy to analyze the National Crime Victimization Survey on a PC even though this is still a very large data set with hundreds of variables and about 60 thousand cases. The student version of SPSS is limited to fifty variables (50) and fifteen hundred cases, but its set-up and manipulation of data sets follows the same principles as the full SPSS package.

The standard format of a data set is such that columns of a data matrix represent variables. Each variable in SPSS has an acronym such as var1, var2, var3, et cetera. (Acronyms used to be limited to eight characters. It is still a good idea to keep them as quite short for ease of typing and because export functions still use short acronyms.) Each variable may include two or more categories with assigned values. If you are collecting your own data you will make the decisions about how to operationalize each variable. If you are using a data set that was collected by someone else, then you will need to read their codebook to understand the representation of **variables** and **values**.

Box 1 Data Matrix of Variables (columns) and Cases (rows)

ID	VAR1	VAR2	VAR3	VAR4	VAR5	Etc.
1	2006	1	16	1	1	
2	2006	2	15	1	1	
...	2006	2	14	3	1	
2000	2006	2	17	3	1	

Box 1 shows a data matrix. The **columns** in the matrix represent **variables**. Variables are the record of what the researcher has measured in his or her study. For example, a variable may be the information about a person's response to a question on a survey. Or, a variable may be more computed by combining information from several variables in a data set to form an index (We will recode variables and compute an index in Chapter 6). The **rows** of a data matrix represent **cases**. Each row contains the information about variables for a particular case. In the example above, we can see that there is an identification variable (ID) and that case number 1 has values of 2006 on variable 1, 1 on variable 2, 16 on variable 3, and so on. The numbers in a data matrix become informative once we know what the variables and cases represent.

There are several ways to create a data matrix in SPSS. The data can be entered directly into the data editor, it can be read in as in-line data as "syntax," or it can be entered into a spreadsheet and imported. We'll do each of these using a very small amount of data.

Let's make up some hypothetical data for an example with six people answering a survey about their fear of crime. This question on fear of crime has been included on several National Crime Surveys asking people "How safe do you (or would you) feel when walking alone at night in your own neighborhood?" Responses to the question are very safe (4), safe (3), unsafe (2), very unsafe (1), and no response (0). We'll also record whether the person is male (M) or female (F). And, we will assign an identification number to each case. The data: Case one is a male who feels safe; case two is a female who feels unsafe; case three is a female who feels safe; case four is a male who feels very safe; case five is a female who feels very unsafe, and case six is a male who refused to tell us how he felt.   We will enter this information into a data matrix.

Now, let's go ahead and start the SPSS for Windows program. I will use the Student version 12.0 in this example. SPSS versions 11 to 13 have very similar windows. The screens in in SPSS 14 may look somewhat different but the features are the same. In Windows, click on the start button, move up to Programs, and down to the SPSS for Windows Student Version icon. A successful start will take you to the default pop-up window asking you "What would you like to do?"

This window is shown in Figure 1.

Click in the circle for "Type in data" and then click on "OK." A new or untitled SPSS data file will be created. The variable names and case numbers are blank.

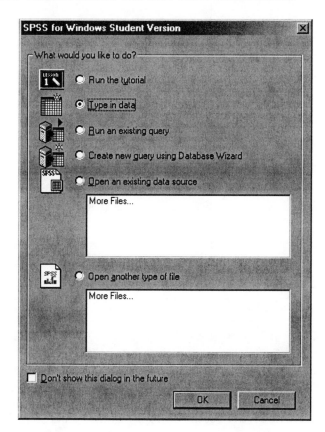

Figure 1 Start-up window for SPSS Student Version 12.0

In SPSS 12, there are "Data view" and "Variable view" tabs at the bottom of the data editor screen. We're going to create two variables and enter some data for each. We will need to define the variables, designate a format, and then label everything! To begin, click on the variable view tab and type "gender" into the top left cell. Figure 2 shows the "variable view" dialogue box.

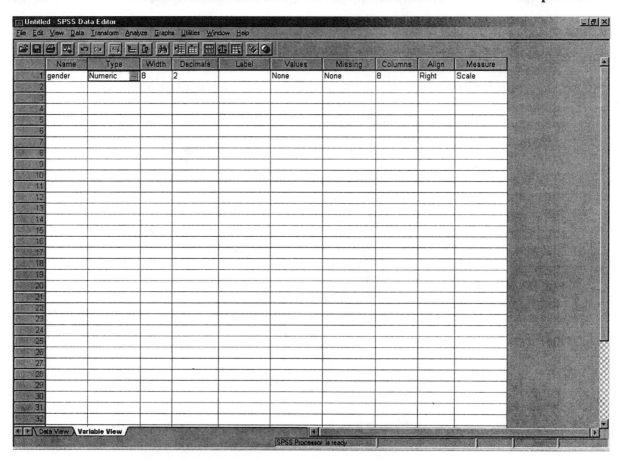

Figure 2   Variable view dialogue box

Note that we will need to set the options on all aspects of variables. Right now, gender is set at the default settings with no labels and a numeric size of 8 wide and 2 decimal places with no labels, no missing values, and so on. Let's change each option to something that is appropriate.

In Chapter 1 we looked at levels of measurement. Note that some of the levels of measurement are shown in Figure 2 as scale, ordinal, and nominal. A user may designate for SPSS procedures the level of measurement of a variable. If you do this, SPSS will attempt to assist you in selecting appropriate statistics. More often, though, most users will not take the time to complete this step. Next, there are several very important settings in this dialogue box: type, labels, and missing values.

There are many types of formats of variables. The most common formats are numeric and string. The numeric form is defined using a fortran code of x.y with x being the number of figures and y being the number of decimal places. The default format for numeric data in SPSS is 8.2. Let's look at our example. How many possibilities are there for gender? That is, how wide can the variable be? The numbers 0-9 have a width of 1, 10 to 99 are 2 figures, 100 to 999 are 3, and so on. Are there any decimal places for gender? No. We'll want to change the TYPE to 1 wide with 0 decimal places. Click on "Type" and do this now.

A second common type of variable is so-called "string" format. String variables are alphanumeric (letters and/or numbers) that may range from 1 to 255 characters. A string format is usually used when letters are an efficient way of operationalizing categories. Examples include the common operationalization of gender as M and F, to typing in of the open-ended responses to a question on a survey, to recording the exact spelling of names of people. For gender, we'd can operationalize male and female as M and F because people easily recognize the categories. For open-ended questions, we'd like an interviewer or data entry person to type the response to the question. My experience with string variables is that they will work for open-ended questions when the response is expected to be relatively short. That is, the response can be typed in 20 to 40 character spaces. If string variables are very long, over the years, it has been my experience that string variables are generally difficult to analyze, or worse yet that they hinder analysis. As such, I try to use numeric variables avoiding string variables when a numeric code can be used. The primary reason for using numeric format is that there are instances where the same variable (e.g. gender) operationalized as a numeric variable can be used in statistical analyses but the string variable cannot be included.

Labeling of variables and their attributes is an important part of data entry. Labels should be **descriptive** and there should be a label for **every attribute** including missing values. The only exception to this rule is that on scales we may want to just label the minimum and maximum values (e.g. Very satisfied [1] to very dissatisfied [7] with intermediate values blank [2 to 6]). Try to avoid the use of abbreviations and acronyms because you may forget what they stand for and they make it difficult for other people to read your work. People do use acronyms in codebooks but they should be avoided. You will see many acronyms in the Monitoring the Future data set that is included with this workbook. In some cases, their use of acronyms is clear and in others it is very difficult to interpret the computer output without going to their codebook. The major goal in using labels is to make the computer output readable for you and for others.

There are two kinds of labels to add to a variable: variable and value labels. Labels should provide a description of the basic content of the variable. Look at figure 2 to find LABEL. For our example, let's label fear as "Feel safe walking at night." Next we need to add labels for Each of the values/categories. Click on values and three dots will appear. Double click on these dots to bring up the "value labels" dialogue box. These are entered one at a time by entering the value, the label, and then clicking on "add." Every possible value including no response (0) should be labeled. Once everything has been entered you will click on continue. These procedures are repeated for every variable.

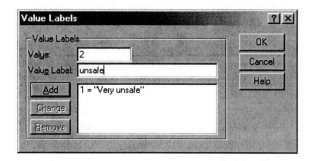

Figure 3 Value Labels dialogue box

The third major feature in defining data is that values of variables may be set as **valid** or **missing**. Statistical analyses will count the number of **valid cases** for a variable. For example, people may refuse to answer a question, or they may not know, or a question may be not applicable. The researcher will want to know the average for people who answered the question, and to know the number of missing cases in his or her statistical analysis. The statistical software must be instructed which responses are to be treated as **missing values**. This is done by clicking on the MISSING tab in the variable view (Figure 2). Missing values may be assigned as specific numbers or as a range of numbers.

A good codebook will inform the user about the assignment of all codes and it will provide information about missing values. For example, in Box 2, GRASS is the variable acronym for whether people in America feel that marijuana should be legalized. Find this question in the codebook. Note that the variable is labeled as "Should marijuana be made legal." Each of the coding categories 0,1, 2, 8 and 9 are labeled, in turn, as NAP, Legal, Not legal, Don't know, and Refused. And, lastly there is an "M" beside the 0, 8, and 9 indicating that these codes are set as missing values and excluded from statistical analysis

Box 2 Valid and missing values from the codebook for the General Social Survey

> **GRASS**   Should marijuana be made legal
> Missing Values: 0, 8, 9
> Value   Label
>   0 M NAP
>   1   LEGAL
>   2   NOT LEGAL
>   8 M DK
>   9 M NA

Figure 4 shows how to define missing values for our variable fear. We want to set zero as a discrete missing value.

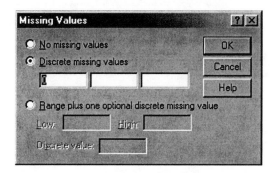

Figure 4   **Missing Values**

Missing values are set by the researcher. You must look to see whether particular values are excluded or should be excluded from statistical analysis of data. Do not assume that these are set properly when you use a data set that has been put together by someone else. In fact, most researchers will turn all missing values off when they archive their data because different statistical packages may treat missing values in different ways. It is up to you as a researcher to ensure that these are set properly.

By now you can see that we have all of the necessary information for defining each of the three variables for our exercise. Try it yourself by creating the variables, adding labels, setting missing values, and then entering all of the data for the six people. When you are complete the data editor should look like the data editor shown in figure 5. Where necessary, you can adjust the width of columns to see variable names by clicking and dragging the border between variables.

For our example, let's assume that we will code gender as male= 1, and female =. Fear will be coded as Very unsafe =1, unsafe = 2, safe = 3, very safe = 4, and no response = 0. The six people for this exercise are:

male and safe	1, 3
female and unsafe	2, 2
female and safe	2, 3
male and very safe	1, 4
female and very unsafe	2, 1
male and no response	1, 0

Enter these data into SPSS and your screen should look like Figure 5 shown on the next page.

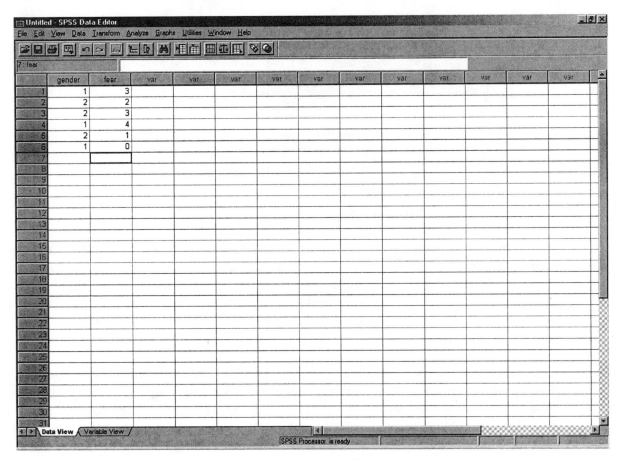

Figure 5 Completed data matrix for example on fear of crime

The real test to see how well you've entered the data and its associated information comes when you produce a frequencies distribution. There should be **labels on everything** and **missing values should be active**. Generate frequency distributions for gender and fear using the same procedures that you used in Chapter 1: Analyze, Descriptive Statistics, Frequencies ....

Figure 6 on the next page shows the computer output.

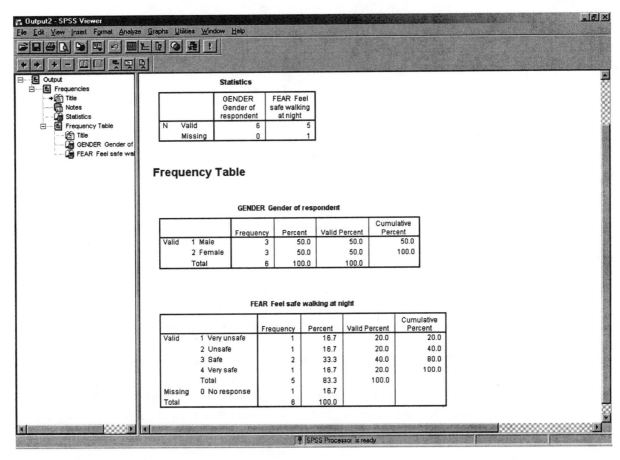

Figure 6 Frequency distributions for gender and fear

These frequency distributions are "clean" with labels on each of the variables and values. A good starting point in any analysis is to look at frequency distributions to ensure that there are no "wildcodes." Wildcodes may be data entry errors where an incorrect value was entered into the computer, or they may be values where a label is needed. It is a normal part of data entry to examine computer output, and to fix these problems.

Putting together a data set can be a lot of work. Thus, you may want to save your data file. This is done from the data editor window by clicking on file, and then save. Figure 7 shows the save data dialogue box.

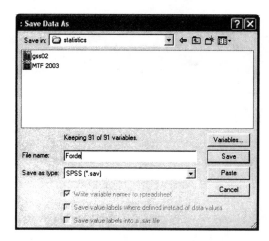

Figure 7 Saving data

The default folder for SPSS student version is a folder called "student." I have moved the location of the file to a folder on my travel drive which I created and called statistics. The file may also be saved on a diskette by changing the save in folder from student to a floppy disk drive (A:).

The default type of file is an SPSS file (.sav). You'll need to name the file in order to save it. It is a good practice to use descriptive names for files so that you may catalog them for later use. I have typed my last name as the File name since this is what I ask students to do when handing in a completed data file. If their name is on it, I know that it is their data file. Putting a unique and descriptive name on your files will help you to keep organized too.

At this point, you have seen all of the necessary steps to create and save an SPSS data file. In the next section, you will see how larger datasets are created and accessed using a syntax window. Information is also provided about the Inter-University Consortium for Political and Social Research.

SPSS Syntax

The SPSS Base manual describes SPSS syntax in much greater detail. These manuals can be purchased from SPSS. While they are moderately expensive, they are useful. Also, these manuals are often available in a reference section of university libraries and/or reference areas in large computer rooms.

What I would like you to see in this example is that there are several key elements in the syntax file that you also create for the same data set when you use the data editor. The data list statement defines the format of variables. The variable and value labels statements add appropriate labels. A missing values statement sets missing values for fear. The begin data and end data statements are used with in-line data. Each statement is ended by a period which tells SPSS to move to the next command. SPSS calls this period a "command terminator."

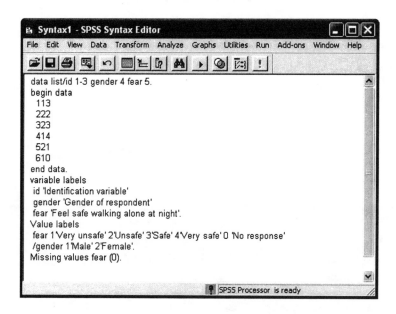

Figure 8   SPSS syntax for our example on fear of crime

Note that SPSS Student Version cannot handle SPSS syntax. You will need to use the full version if you wish to try using the syntax window for this exercise. The importance of knowing about SPSS syntax is that it is used to activate many of the large data sets that are archived by the Inter-University Consortium for Political and Social Research (ICPSR). SPSS syntax statements can be read by the full SPSS software including the graduate package and career starter, and each version uses the same basic syntax.

DATA LIBRARIES

Another important source of data files is the Inter-University Consortium for Political and Social Research (ICPSR). Many federally funded projects have a requirement that the data from the project be archived in a format that can be accessed by other people. ICPSR data librarians have taken peoples' data sets and saved the raw data, SPSS syntax, and/or SAS syntax. Their hard work means that you have access to many data sets in the ICPSR data library. If you are considering a term paper, thesis, or advanced research project you may want to access a data file from the ICPSR library.

Importantly, you now know that someone had to spend the time to enter these data, add variable and value labels, and set missing values. It is still quite a bit of work to prepare a data set from a data library, but it is a valuable resource potentially saving you the time that it took to collect the original data, and the cost is low (in fact FREE to most users).

Figure 9 shows the entrance window to the National Archive of Criminal Justice Data. This is a topical archive at the Inter-university Consortium of Political and Social Research which is located at the University of Michigan in Ann Arbor, Michigan. You can access it on the world wide web at: www.icpsr.umich.edu. The National Archive of Criminal Justice Data is one of the topical archives at ICPSR.

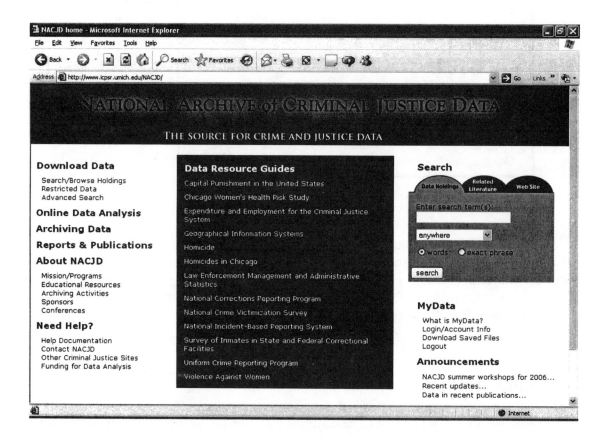

Figure 9 The National Archive of Criminal Justice Data

There are several ways to find materials in this data library. You may search or browse holdings by clicking on the link on the left side of the screen. Or, you can enter words or phases in the Search box on the right side of the screen. I chose to enter "terrorism" into the search box which generated the screen shown below as "Search results."

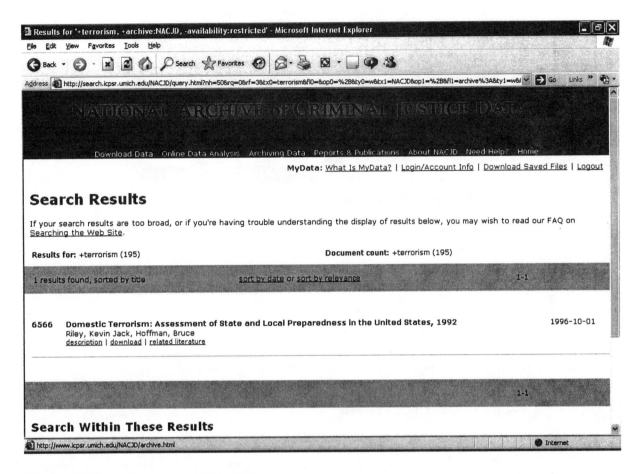

Figure 10 Search screen at NACJD

The search shown in Figure 10 yielded only one title. If more results are found then it is sorted by title. It may also be sorted by date. Note the links at the bottom of each study. You may learn more about each study by clicking on "description." The download link will take you directly to a download screen. The related literature link provides a listing of publications based on the particular dataset. When you're starting a library search, you'll most likely want to read more about a study before downloading it. Let's have a look at the description for ICPSR study 6566.

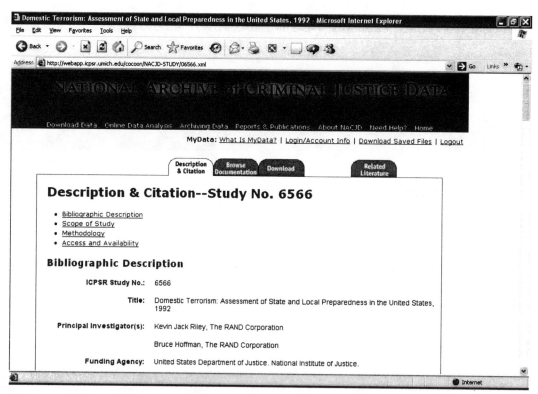

Figure 11 Description screen

Notice that the description gives you a very large amount of information about each study including who did it, who funded it, the methodology, and the access to files and their availability. In particular, we would like to know what the study is about and to find out about the format of the data files, whether there is an on-line codebook, and the structure of the data set(s).

An ICPSR abstract gives a brief description of the purpose of the project. At the end of them, they also provide references where additional published information about the study can be found. Most data sets also have on-line (machine readable) documentation of codebooks and questionnaire instruments (if applicable). This extent of documentation about the collection of data is described under the heading "Extent of the collection."

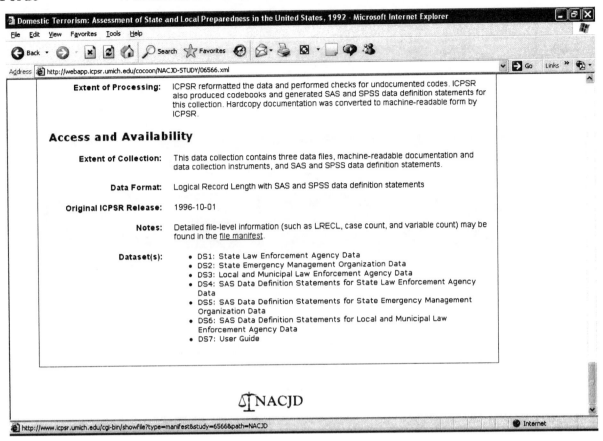

Figure 12 Bottom section of description screen

The extent of collection tells us that there are data files, codebooks, questionnaires and importantly that there are SAS and SPSS data definition statements. The access and availability section is very important. You should be looking for information about documentation and statistical software. Above it tells you that there are SPSS and SAS data definition statements (syntax). This study has three data files, a PDF user guide, a codebook, data collection instruments in PDF, and SAS and SPSS data definition statements. Note that the full version of SPSS can easily handle these files.

The availability of some files is restricted to ICPSR member institutions. If your college is a member of ICPSR, your college library should be able to tell you how to obtain permission to access these restricted data files.

Next, we would like to download the data. Go back to the search screen and click on downloads (see Figure 10) or click on the download tab (see Figure 11). A permissions screen will pop-up (Figure 13). Many ICPSR data sets are available for free to the general public for research purposes. The permissions procedures require that you provide some information about yourself and a declaration of how you will use the data. ICPSR may ask you to complete a brief questionnaire asking you who you are, where you are located, and what you plan to do with the data.

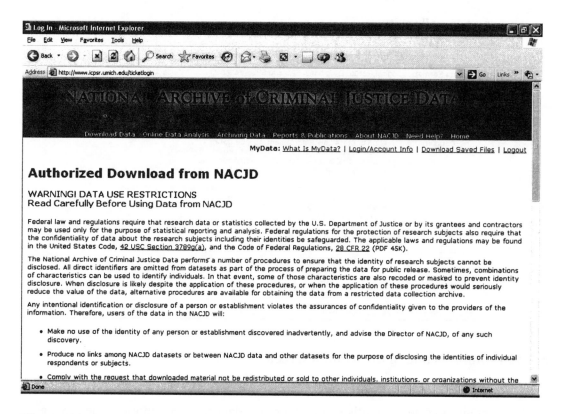

Figure 13 Permissions screen

The final steps to putting together a data set involve selecting the files that you need to download. The main items are documentation (codebook or questionnaires), raw data, and data definition statements (SPSS, SAS, et cetera). Figure 14 shows that I selected all files and all datasets. The third step is "add to data cart." This will put the files in a cart and tell you how large the files are going to be. Figure 15 shows that ICPSR prepares a compressed file for downloading.

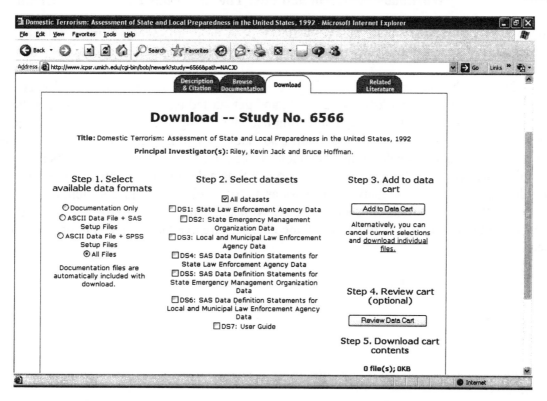

Figure 14 Data screen at NACJD

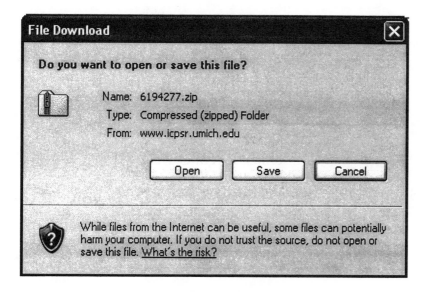

Figure 15 Download screen at NACJD

I chose to save the file and placed it on my desktop. A program such as Winzip will be needed in order to open this file.

Now you've seen where some of the data came from for this work-book. You could select your own study, download a codebook, and get started on using SPSS to access the data. Just keep in mind that putting a large and complex data set together may require persistence and patience. Also, many data sets are quite large so that they will not fit on a floppy disk. It may take some planning to download the codebook. Check to see whether the variables that you need are in the data set. And, from there, download SPSS data definition statements, the data, note the variables you need, and lastly save your work as an SPSS file. The SPSS system files (.sav files) are smaller than the raw data files shown in the syntax statements. It can be a lot of work to get to this point but research is hard work and the data sets are available for you to use in your research.

KEY TERMS

Codebook
Data library
Data view
Missing values
Syntax
Value labels
Variable labels
Variable view

Web-sites

www.icpsr.umich.edu   Inter-university Consortium for Political and Social Research

www.spss.com   Statistical Package for the Social Sciences, Inc.

Name _____   Date _____

Research Problems;

1.   Construct a data set based on the following hypothetical data. These data represent a summary of the interviewer's observations and people's opinions about their favorite thing to do downtown on a summer evening in Bigtown, USA. The interviewer asks people about their favorite activity, notes their sex, and asks them about their age.

Your job is to take the respondent's opinion and the interviewer's observations to make a dataset which can be used to summarize public opinion about downtown activities in Bigtown, USA. Variables include gender (male [1]; female [2]), the person's approximate age in years, and what they like to do downtown: (restaurants [1], casino [2], professional baseball [3], live bands [4], other [5], and don't know [8]). Code missing information in all questions as a zero [0].

On this sheet, assign an ID number to each line, assign numbers to each category, and then use these numbers to complete the data entry. The data for each interview are:

- Gamble big-time, Male, 25 years old
- We like to check out the bands, Female, 29
- Baseball. Go team! Male 50
- I have no idea, Female, 30
- Get lost buddy, Male, refused age
- Casinos. Male, 30
- Get drunk. Male, 23
- Have a few beers at the game, Male, 20
- Baseball, Female, 18
- A casino, Female, 75
- My wife and I like to dine downtown, Male, 45
- Take my wife and kids to the game, Male, 35
- Casinos since you get "free" drinks, Male, 25
- I don't know. I'm new in town. Female, 30
- Live bands and no cover-charge, Female, 20
- A casino of course! Male, 30
- I love the restaurants, Female, 20
- Baseball, Male, 20
- I don't know, I don't go downtown very often, Female, 25
- Drinking down by the river, Male, 25

Name _____   **Date** _____

Tasks
- Use the data window to create your data set.
- Ensure that all variables and values are labeled.
- Save the data set on a diskette using your name as the name of the file (e.g. Forde.sav).
- For each variable, generate the frequency distribution.

Write the frequency distribution for people's opinion about their favorite activity in the summer in downtown of Bigtown, USA.

Write a brief interpretation of these results.

Name _____   **Date** _____

2.   Design a short questionnaire that includes two questions.

Tasks
- Write out hypothetical answers to the above questions for twenty-five respondents.
- Use the data window to create your data set.
- Ensure that all variables and values are labeled.
- Save the data set on a diskette using a different name for the file (e.g. Forde Q2.sav).
- For each variable, generate a frequency distribution.

Interpretation: You will need to ensure that the completed frequency distribution provides the reader with the complete information for each variable.

Name _____   **Date** _____

The following questions will require "going an extra mile."

3.   Go to the Inter-University Consortium for Political and Social Research.

   1. Find a data set that interests you.
   2. Print the Abstract
   3. Determine the extent of documentation, and whether SPSS can be used to access the data.

4. Go to the General Social Survey Web-site: www.icpsr.umich.edu in the topical archives.

   1. Find two variables of interest to you.
   2. Print their codebook information.
   3. Extract these two variables including the codebooks, raw data and SPSS data definition statements. These files are generated in compressed format. Save the compressed file to a travel drive or hard drive. Use WinZip to decompress this file. Use the syntax window in SPSS to execute the commands. You must change the filename in the syntax file to note the physical location of the files. This is the directory on your travel drive or hard drive. *This part is a difficult task for a novice but it is not impossible!*

RECODING AND COMPUTING NEW VARIABLES

INTRODUCTION

You may wish to come back to the exercises for this chapter later when you are more familiar with data analysis. It would be useful, nonetheless, to read over the examples in this chapter to learn about some of the reasons for recoding and transforming variables. Whether you're working with a data file that someone else has created or one of your own making, variables in a data file often need to be recoded in some way, or values for new variables need to be calculated based on changes in the old variables.

Some of the main reasons to recode variables are:

1. You want to change the order of the categories so that the values go from what is intuitively the lowest to highest.
2. You may have two studies that have similar variables but different coding schemes. You might recode to make them as comparable as possible.
3. You may want to recode so that you use a different statistic or procedure.
4. You may wish to recode to collapse or group a large number of categories into a few categories.
5. A recode and computation may allow you to look at combinations across several variables.

EXAMPLE 1: Reordering categories

The General Social Survey asked the following question in 2004:

CAPPUN   Favor or oppose death penalty for murder
    Missing Values: 0, 8, 9
    Value   Label
      0 M NAP
      1   FAVOR
      2   OPPOSE
      8 M DK
      9 M NA

We might want to change the order on this question to include persons who say they don't know as a category between favor and oppose. How about favor (1), neutral (don't know as 2), and oppose as (3)?

The frequency distribution for the original coding is shown below:

CAPPUN FAVOR OR OPPOSE DEATH PENALTY FOR MURDER

		Frequency	Percent	Valid Percent	Cumulative Percent
Valid	1 FAVOR	444	29.6	67.4	67.4
	2 OPPOSE	215	14.3	32.6	100.0
	Total	659	43.9	100.0	
Missing	0 NAP	790	52.7		
	8 DK	45	3.0		
	9 NA	6	.4		
	Total	841	56.1		
Total		1500	100.0		

To recode, click on **TRANSFORM**, then click on **RECODE**, and then click on recode **INTO DIFFERENT VARIABLES**. It is a good idea to create a new variable rather than writing over the original (variable) because you may wish to keep the original variable for other analyses and you should verify that the changes were correct.

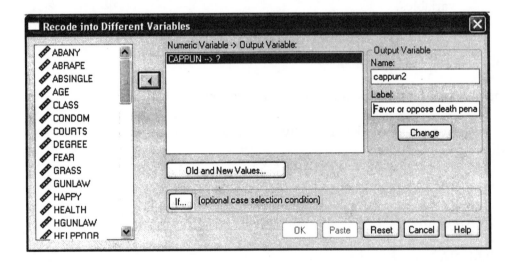

You can call the output variable anything you like. I put a "2" on the end of the original name to denote it as something "recoded." It is a good idea to put a variable label on it too. Click on "Change" to make the new variable.

Next, we are going to have to specify each of the old and new values. You must state the old and new values even if they are to stay the same. If you do not specify a particular category it will be set to system missing.

The screen below shows that 1's will be 3's, 3's will be 2's and 2's will be 1's. Enter each of the values into the old value box and the new value box, and then click "Add."

Notice that you could specify a range of old values to be recoded into a single new value. Click on "Continue" when you have all values entered which will take you back to the recode screen.

Click on "OK" to complete the recoding of CAPPUN into a new variable CAPPUN2.

Using the FREQUENCIES procedure, the distribution for the new variable is shown below. Notice that new variables are added to the end of the data file (or alphabetically if your options are set for alphabetical).

cappun2 Favor or oppose death penalty

		Frequency	Percent	Valid Percent	Cumulative Percent
Valid	1.00	444	29.6	63.1	63.1
	2.00	45	3.0	6.4	69.5
	3.00	215	14.3	30.5	100.0
	Total	704	46.9	100.0	
Missing	System	796	53.1		
Total		1500	100.0		

Compare the new values to the original frequency distribution. There were 444 people who said they favored the death penalty (1) in the original table and there are 444 that show as 1's in this table. Check each of the other categories to see that the recode is correct. We're not done yet as it is important to label each of the categories. Go to the variable view in SPSS and add labels for each of the categories. Also, notice that values which were set to missing in the original variable are grouped together and shown as system missing in the new table. If you need to keep the information from the original table, you would need to include these numbers (0 and 9) in the recode statement.

A complete frequency distribution is shown below.

cappun2 Favor or oppose death penalty

		Frequency	Percent	Valid Percent	Cumulative Percent
Valid	1 Favor	444	29.6	63.1	63.1
	2 Neutral	45	3.0	6.4	69.5
	3 Oppose	215	14.3	30.5	100.0
	Total	704	46.9	100.0	
Missing	System	796	53.1		
Total		1500	100.0		

What is the level of measurement of the original coding of the variable? And what is it for the new coding scheme? The answers are nominal and then ordinal. Simply changing the coding of this variable will change the types of statistics that can be used with it.

EXAMPLE 2: Collapsing some categories

The Monitoring the Future Study measured heroin use in the past 30 days as an ordinal variable with the following categories:

v141 042R* :#X "H"/LAST30DA

		Frequency	Percent	Valid Percent	Cumulative Percent
Valid	1 0 OCCAS:(1)	1446	96.4	99.3	99.3
	2 1-2X:(2)	5	.3	.3	99.7
	3 3-5X:(3)	1	.1	.1	99.7
	5 10-19X:(5)	1	.1	.1	99.8
	7 40+OCCAS:(7)	3	.2	.2	100.0
	Total	1456	97.1	100.0	
Missing	-9 MISSING	44	2.9		
Total		1500	100.0		

Given that there are very few high school students that have used heroin, we might want to recode the variable so that all persons who have used it are combined and shown as Yes (1) and students that have not are shown as no (0). To do this we would recode 2 through 7 as 1 and 1 as 0.

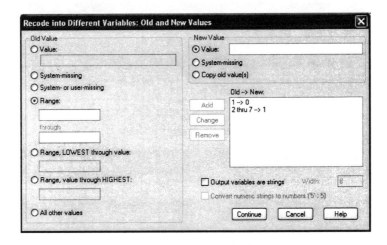

The frequency distribution for the recoded variable shows that less than 1 percent of American high school seniors have tried heroin in the past 30 days. This is a nominal variable.

v141r Heroin use in past 30 days

		Frequency	Percent	Valid Percent	Cumulative Percent
Valid	0 No	1446	96.4	99.3	99.3
	1 Yes	10	.7	.7	100.0
	Total	1456	97.1	100.0	
Missing	System	44	2.9		
Total		1500	100.0		

EXAMPLE 3: Grouping categories

The General Social Survey asks people about the number of hours of television that they watch per day. It is measured as hours per day. Analyzing this kind of variable can lead to very large frequency tables. We want to collapse the categories into just a few groups and analyze this new grouping.

You should have some reason for grouping of categories. I suspect that people who watch no television are different than people who watch some t.v. and from persons who watch a lot. I will group categories as none (0 hours), some (1 to 3 hours), and a lot (4 through the highest valid number).

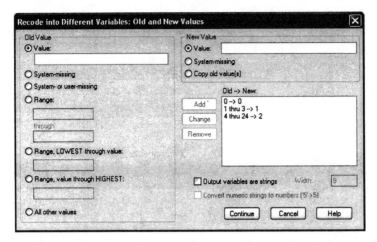

The grouped frequency distribution with labels is shown below. It is very important to label variables to assist you in remembering how categories have been grouped and to assist the reader in seeing what you have done in your analysis.

TVRecode Television viewing

		Frequency	Percent	Valid Percent	Cumulative Percent
Valid	0 None	30	2.0	6.4	6.4
	1 1-3 hours	303	20.2	65.0	71.5
	2 4 or more	133	8.9	28.5	100.0
	Total	466	31.1	100.0	
Missing	System	1034	68.9		
Total		1500	100.0		

EXAMPLE 4 : Computing a new variable

Sometimes we would like to combine two or more variables into one new variable. We've all done this as we add up different scores on a test to get a total. There are many different arithmetic operators that can be used to combine sets of variables. We're just going to look at adding up two variables.

The General Social Survey asks people whether or not it was okay for a police officer to strike a person in different situations. In one instance (POLABUSE, they are asked about a situation where a person is saying vulgar or obscene things to the officer. In another (POLATTAK), the citizen is attacking the policeman with his fists. The coding categories on these variables are yes (1) and no (2). We would like to know how many people say yes to both questions, yes on one question, and no on all questions. What would a "yes" and "yes" add up to? The answer is 2. Combining no and no will add to 4. One no and one yes will add to 3. We can compute a new variable that will help us to analyze the combined responses.

Click on TRANSFORM and then COMPUTE. We will name a new (target) variable and then tell it how it is to be calculated. In this instance we will add POLABUSE to POLATTAK to create a new variable which will be called POLTOT. Values that were set to missing are not included in the new variable and these will be set to system missing in the new variable.

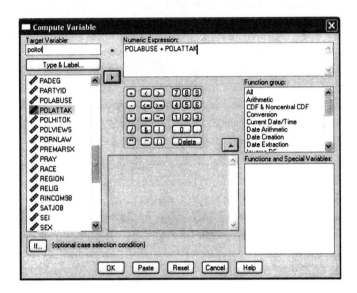

The frequency distribution for the combined variable is shown below. I have added a variable label and value labels using the variable view in the data editor.

poltot Okay for office to use force when citizen is saying vulgar things or citizen is attacking officer

		Frequency	Percent	Valid Percent	Cumulative Percent
Valid	2 Yes on both	35	2.3	7.8	7.8
	3 Yes on one	373	24.9	83.6	91.5
	4 No on both	38	2.5	8.5	100.0
	Total	446	29.7	100.0	
Missing	System	1054	70.3		
Total		1500	100.0		

SUMMARY

In later chapters, you will see instances where it may be useful to recode or combine variables. Keep in mind that it is a good idea to create a new variable when recoding so that you can verify that the recoding was done properly. Variable and value labels are important as well. In a more advanced class, you may see that these same steps can easily be done in the syntax editor.

Importantly, if you wish to keep new variables (recoded or computed) you must save the changes to your file. If you do not need the file you may discard it. Note that if you make a mistake with a data file for this workbook you can download it again from the web-site or copy it from a co-student's file.

KEY TERMS

Compute
Group values
Recode

Name _____   **Date** _____

Complete the following problems.

1. Using the General Social Survey, recode AGE into four different age groups.

    a. What groupings will you use and why?

    b. Label each of the new groups

    c. Generate a frequency distribution and write it below:

2. Using the General Social Survey, recode COURTS with "about right" moved to the middle of the distribution and "not harsh enough" moved to the end. What was the original level of measurement? What is it now?

3. Using the Monitoring the Future Study, compute a new variable to identify whether high school students have ever drank alcohol (V103) **and** ever smoked marijuana or hashish (V115). Note that you will have to recode v115 into a yes (1) or no (2) format before computing the combined variable.

    a. What is the range in values for the new variable? _____ to _____

    b. Write the frequency distribution below:

4. Select a key question from one of the surveys. Using your college library, find a research article on the same topic; or find a similar question on one of the other surveys in this workbook. Identify the similarities / differences in how the variables are measured. If different, can the variables be recoded so that results from the studies could be compared.

GRAPHING DATA

INTRODUCTION

In Chapter 1A we looked at frequency distributions. The strength of a frequency table is that it may provide detailed information about a variable whether it is counts, percentages, valid percentages or even the amount of missing data. A weakness, however, is that large tables can lead to information overload where a reader is overwhelmed by the information and he or she doesn't see the key point in a table. Graphs provide a method to visually present information from a table to highlight an important statistic or trend.

A graph is defined as a pictorial representation of a table to show variation in one variable, or differences across groups or time. Graphs aid in the interpretation of complex tables. Nonetheless, there is a trade off to be made when using a graph versus a table. We gain visual emphasis but we lose precision that was provided in the table.

This chapter introduces you to three types of graphs: pie chart, bar chart, and line graph. Additionally, this chapter will explain how to effectively display a graph and how to transform several kinds of tables into graphs.

To choose a graphical device, it is important to know the level of measurement of a variable and the number of categories or values in it. Pie and bar charts are used with nominal and ordinal level variables. As the number of categories increases, it is also more likely that a user will move from a pie chart (2-5 categories) to a bar chart. Line graphs are used with interval and ratio level variables.

PIE CHARTS

The purpose of a pie chart is to show the entire distribution of cases across categories. All categories are shown and the graph can be designed to emphasize a particular "slice" of the pie

For example, we might wonder how about the physical health of Americans. The General Social Survey includes a variable on people's self-reports about their happiness. The frequency distribution for happiness (Happy), in two parts, is shown on the next page.

This frequency table provides a detailed summary of the information from the 2004 General Social Survey. It is a complex table which tells us about each of the valid categories on the variable (those people that told us about the condition of their health), people who didn't know or refused to answer the question. There is also a "NAP" category. This category is people who were in the survey but they were not asked this question on their version of the survey. Recall, also, that the instructional data set is a subset of 1500 cases from the entire study designed so that SPSS Student Version may be used to analyze these data. Nonetheless, the instructional data set is designed to be interpreted as a sample of all Americans in 2004.

Statistics

HAPPY GENERAL HAPPINESS

N	Valid	707
	Missing	793

HAPPY GENERAL HAPPINESS

		Frequency	Percent	Valid Percent	Cumulative Percent
Valid	1 VERY HAPPY	240	16.0	33.9	33.9
	2 PRETTY HAPPY	372	24.8	52.6	86.6
	3 NOT TOO HAPPY	95	6.3	13.4	100.0
	Total	707	47.1	100.0	
Missing	0 NAP	790	52.7		
	8 DK	2	.1		
	9 NA	1	.1		
	Total	793	52.9		
Total		1500	100.0		

Figure 1 presents a basic pie chart to show what people said about the condition of health. By taking the frequency table and presenting it as a pie chart, you should be able to quickly visualize the relative percentages of a population that fall into each category.

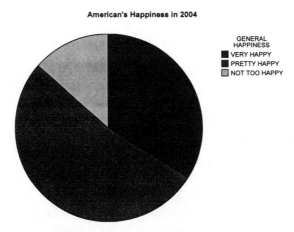

Does this chart catch your eye? It actually needs quite a bit more work done to it in order to meet minimal requirements for providing information. I'm going to take slices out of it to emphasize how many Americans are unhappy. Think about what you might emphasize. What happens to the presentation if "very happy" is emphasized? Remember, when you are making a chart that you are directing the reader of a report to something you would like them to read.

Figure 1. American's Happiness in 2004

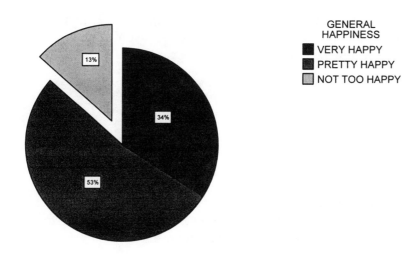

Source: General Social Survey, 2004

N=707 Missing=3

The slice for not too happy represents about 13 percent of the pie. Thus it is quite easy to see that very few Americans say they are not too happy.

Next, look at the footnote that is added. The N is the total number of valid cases. The missing data is the total of DK and NA (2+1=3). You'll need to do this computation when you use the GSS. The total for Missing is normally provided in the Statistics table for the frequency distributions (look above). The percentages for each category are added into the slices by clicking on the slice and getting it to "show data labels" and changing the number of decimal places to zero.

A good graphical device has several features:

- Be large enough that it is easy to read
- A descriptive title
- A listing on the source of information
- The valid N and missing information should be shown
- Each slice should have a short yet descriptive label, or use a legend box

- Percentages for each slice should be shown. Sometimes when there is a large number of categories, it is not possible to include these without "cluttering" the graph.

SPSS can be used to produce graphs. If you have access to the actual dataset you can use it to generate the information. In other cases, you may want to make a new dataset and simply enter the basic information. We will do this with a line graph.

To make the pie chart for praying, open the General Social Survey data set using SPSS. From here, look to the top line beside ANALYZE to click on "Graphs," and move down to Pie. The following dialogue box will appear.

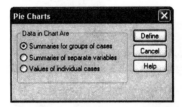

The basic pie chart provides a summary for groups of cases on a single variable. Click on define to produce the main dialogue box. We are going to select HAPPY as our variable and we will tell it to define slices by % of cases.

We can enter some additional information at this point. By default, the program presents N of cases. Since we are more interested in the population of Americans than the sample itself, change this to percentages by clicking on "% of cases." The program by default will show the "valid percentages." In some graphs is may be important to show groups defined by missing values. You can select these "missing" groups by clicking on Options and selecting them.

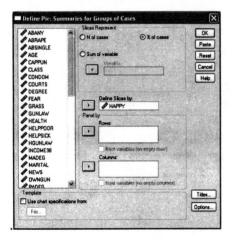

Try both methods and you'll see the difference.

A title and footnotes can be added using the "Titles" box on the lower right of the screen. They can also be added at a later stage. Go ahead, type in the information used in our example to duplicate the pie chart for Figure 1. Click on OK and it will generate a basic pie chart.

Notice that SPSS generates pie charts using color fills, and labels that were brought in from the SPSS file. Note that the percentages for each category are missing, colors are used rather than patterns, and the footnote is centered rather than left justified. Double click on the graph and the Chart editor will open. In this editor, you may click on footnote (or click where the footnote should be) to edit it, click on each label to edit and change options, change the title, change fill patterns, and much more. You can save your chart onto a diskette and make additional changes using SPSS similar to what you would with a regular word processing file when you make revisions. You can also copy the completed chart as a picture into Microsoft word, Word Perfect, or Works. (Hint: you can impress your professor with a neat figure in a report).

BAR CHARTS

Bar charts are an effective way to show how a group (or groups) may differ on a statistic. Most often it is a valid percentage that is shown, but a bar chart can be used with means and rates. You may have seen a bar chart presenting crime rates for different cities, states, or different age groups.

An example of a bar chart is a compilation of a table on fatal traffic accidents in Memphis that I did for the Memphis Police Department. The police had a number of concerns about traffic enforcement and accidents.

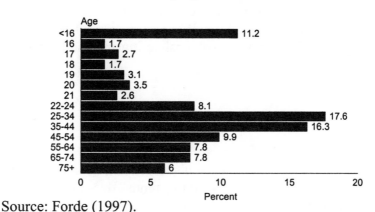

Fatal Traffic Accidents in Memphis, 1989-95
by Age of Victim

Source: Forde (1997).

51

Bar charts are effective because they allow a more precise presentation of information, and they can be used for a relatively large number of categories. The length of the bar is used to portray the amount of the statistic. A bar chart is used to show the specific values for each age group. It can also be used to compare percentages between groups.

This horizontal bar graph shows specific information about victims between the ages of 16 and 21 and grouped information for other age groups. This was done to meet a request for detailed information on young drivers.

Bar charts are easily produced using SPSS using the GRAPH procedure. The basic bar chart is a "simple" bar chart. The initial dialogue box is shown below.

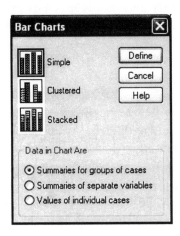

Clustered bar charts are used when you want to make comparisons on a distribution based on a second variable. For example, you might want to compare fatal traffic accident information broken down for males and females. Stacked bar charts are a more complex bar chart which is used when you want to compare distributions across groups. The stacked bar chart provides an alternative to using several charts when you wish to illustrate and compare distributions across groups.

LINE GRAPHS

Line graphs are used to examine the distribution in an interval or ratio level variable. Line graphs are very often used to demonstrate "trends" over time. They can also be used to compare two or more groups on the same graph.

For example, we might want to graph the violent crime rate in the United States. The frequency table is drawn from the Uniform Crime Reports that are published by the FBI. The violent crime rate is a rate per 100,000 persons. We will need to enter this information into SPSS. This is a very easy task to do.

Start SPSS, create two variables (Year and VCR), and then type the information into two data columns. The information from the Uniform Crime Reports follows:

Year:	Violent Crime Rate		
1985	556.6	1995	684.6
1986	617.7	1996	636.5
1987	609.7	1997	611.3
1988	637.2	1998	567.5
1989	663.1	1999	524.7
1990	731.8	2000	506.5
1991	758.1	2001	504.5
1992	757.5	2002	494.4
1993	746.8	2003	475.8
1994	713.6	2004	465.5

Once you have the data into the SPSS file, double check that you've entered the data properly. Next, go to "Graphs", select a line chart to bring up the dialogue box. In this instance, we are going to produce a simple line chart based on the values of the cases.   The dialogue box follows:

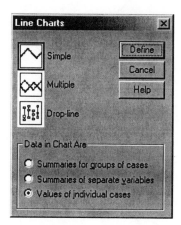

Move the variables over so that the line will represent the violent crime rate and the category labels will be the year.

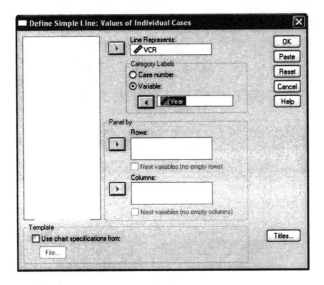

You can also add a title and source at this point. The resulting line graph shows the trend in the violent crime rate in the United States over the period 1985 to 2004.

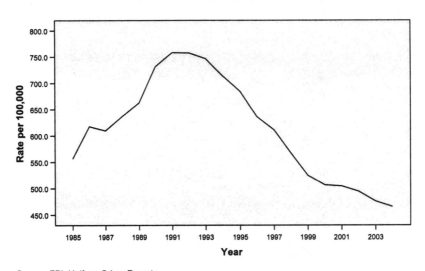

A few additional changes were made to the graph using the graphics editor. First, the label VCR was changed to read as a rate per 100,000. Second, the labels for year were modified so that only every second year was shown and the Source was left-aligned.

The resulting line graph clearly shows that the violent crime rate peaked about 1992 and it has declined substantially since so that in 2004 it is at its lowest point over the entire period of 1985 to 2004.

There are additional issues that could be considered for this graph. Should the scale for the violent crime rate go from zero to 800? SPSS will choose values for a scale that go from the lowest value to the highest value.

Violent Crime in the United States, 1985-2004

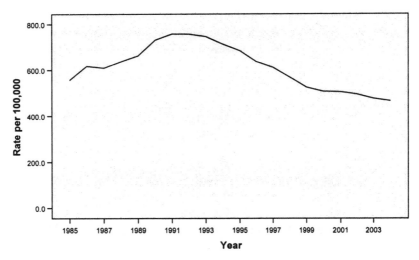

Source: FBI, Uniform Crime Reports

A rate of 450 for a start can potentially be misleading though. With the higher starting point, the declines look steeper. With a zero starting point for the violent crime rate, the graph looks flatter. What would happen if you chose to only report violent crime for the past ten years? Also, should we choose a longer time frame such as back to 1950, or 1960? How far back in time can we go using the Uniform Crime Reports? The point of these questions is that you will have to make a decision about what scale you wish to show on your graph and that your choice can influence how people view the information.

FEATURES OF A GOOD GRAPH

- A title
- Nominal and ordinal level variables
  - Pie chart (if few categories)
  - Bar chart (if many)
- Interval and ratio level variables
  - Bar chart (discrete metric)
  - Line chart (discrete or continuous)
- Label slices, bars, lines, and axes
- Show percentages (if visually possible)
- Report N's
- Cite Source(s)

KEY WORDS

Bar chart
Pie chart
Line chart

Web-sites

The most recent volumes of the Federal Bureau of Investigation's Uniform Crime Reports can be read on-line:

    www.fbi.gov

The *Sourcebook of Criminal Justice Statistics* has many tables that are of interest to social researchers.

    www.albany.edu/sourcebook

Name _____   **Date** _____

Tasks/Interpretation: Fill in the blank for each variable.

1. Select an appropriate graphical device for the following variables. Refer to the codebooks for information on each variable. You must determine the level of measurement for each variable. **This task can and should be completed before you go to a computer lab.**
2. Produce a graphical device for each variable. Print the resulting graph and attach it to your homework (if requested).
3. Write a brief interpretation of the graphical device in the space provided.

Use the Monitoring the Future Study to graph:

1. The valid percentages for how students perceive the risk of trying crack cocaine once or twice (v1773).

Use the Monitoring the Future Study to graph:

2.   The self-reported grade distribution of high school seniors in 2004 (v179).

Name _____   **Date** _____

Use the Monitoring the Future survey:

3.   Select a variable and choose an appropriate graphical device.

Name _____   **Date** _____

Use the General Social Survey:

4.   Make a horizontal bar graph of total family income in American in 2004 (incom98). Note that this income for people in 2004 is converted into 1998 dollars so that results can be compared across surveys.

Name _____   **Date** _____

The following data is excerpted from Table 2.90 of the Sourcebook for Criminal Justice Statistics. A nationally representative sample of college freshmen were asked whether or not marijuana should be legal. These data are the percentages indicating "yes."

Year	Total	Male	Female
1995	33.4	37.1	30.3
1996	32.4	36.1	29.4
1997	33.1	36.7	30.1
1998	32.7	37.7	28.6
1999	32.4	37.2	28.4
2000	34.2	40.4	29.1
2001	36.5	42.9	31.4
2002	39.7	45.8	34.7
2003	38.8	44.3	34.3
2004	37.2	43.1	32.5

Maguire, K. & Pastore, A.L. (Eds.) (2006) *Sourcebook of Criminal Justice Statistics* [Online]. Available: http://www.albany.edu/sourcebook/pdf/t290.pdf [July 10, 2006].

5. Produce a line graph for one of these trends. Label it and interpret the trend. If you care to go the extra mile, locate the Sourcebook online to get additional information about the original sources used to compile this table.

Name _____   **Date** _____

6.   Using the General Social Survey, what kind of graphical device would you recommend for age in years (Age)? Explain your choice.

7.   Recode age into four age groups and produce a pie-chart.

MEASURES OF CENTRAL TENDENCY

INTRODUCTION

There are three commonly used measures of central tendency: mode, median, and mean. The mode is simply the most common score, the median is the middle case in a distribution, and the mean is the arithmetic average.

The shape of a distribution, however, can influence whether the mean is an appropriate statistic. Unusual scores will distort a distribution from "normal" and when this happens we select the median as a better measure than the mean. It is also important to evaluate the shape of a distribution because many statistics assume that a variable is normally distributed.

If a distribution is symmetric, the mean and median will be the same value. If a distribution is positively skewed, the mean will be pulled to the right. If it is negatively skewed, the mean will be pulled to the left. If a distribution is skewed, the median will fall between the mode and the mean and the median will be a better measure of the average. We can look at a bar chart and make our best guess about whether to use the mean or the median.

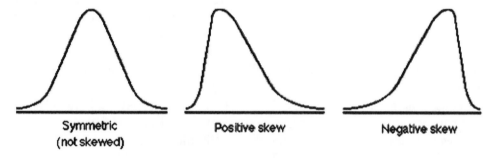

Symmetric
(not skewed)   Positive skew   Negative skew

Figure 1   Skewness

For example, suppose that we have a summer class with 20 students in it. The combined income of 19 of them is $80,000 and we have "Super Dunk" (a Basketball Player making about 5 million dollars a year). The mean income for the entire class is $254,000. Is it reasonable to say the average income of students is $254,000? No! The distribution is skewed to the right by an outlying case so that the median value of $4500 is a better measure of the average.

In social science research we also have to assess the shape of distributions. Marvin Wolfgang and his colleagues long ago showed us that a small number of juveniles commit the vast majority of delinquent acts. How about the average for police use of excessive force? Fortunately, it is relatively unusual. Or, fear of crime? Extremely high levels of fear occur but they also are unusual.

The objectives of this chapter are to introduce measures of central tendency and to demonstrate how the shape of the distribution of a variable may influence measures of central tendency. In particular, you will look to see how the mean of a distribution may be biased by the skew of a distribution. You will:

1. look at the shape of a distribution using a histogram;
2. guess whether the median or the mean is larger; and
3. compare your estimate from the histogram to the actual values.

DATA ANALYSIS

In Chapter 1A you generated a table of the frequency distribution for a number of variables. Graphic presentations can also be effectively used to illustrate the shape of a distribution. A reader can see where scores fall and can estimate what the average score is in a distribution. Bar graphs and line graphs are commonly used to examine interval (or ordinal variables when we make an assumption that can be treated as interval level) and ratio level variables. These variables are treated as if they were continuous to emphasize continuity along the length of a scale. Usually, the values of a variable are grouped into class intervals of equal size. For example, hours of t.v. watching could alternatively be grouped into half- hour intervals; or age could be grouped in five, ten, or one year intervals.

The histograms in SPSS look very much like the bar charts you saw in the last chapter. They are generated as a "chart" in the FREQUENCIES procedure. In a histogram, the relative length of the bar equals the relative frequency for the class interval. By looking at the shape of the histogram we can get an idea of skewedness (symmetry) and peakedness (or kurtosis) of a distribution. We would like to know whether the distribution is symmetric or skewed, and whether the kurtosis is flat, peaked, or normal. Today we will just consider whether a variable is skewed or normal. Again, the reason to conduct this analysis is that we want to know whether the mean is an appropriate statistic for a distribution.

The distribution of a variable is symmetrical when scores look the same on both sides of the middle. A distribution is asymmetrical when scores fall to one side or the other. When there is a substantial difference in movement of scores we call this a skewed distribution. A distribution is a positive (or right-tail) skew when extreme scores fall to the right of center. A distribution is negative (or left-tail) when extreme scores fall to the left of center. For example, most high school students tend to feel safe at school. The distribution of cases is left-skewed as few students feel very dissatisfied with their personal safety at school. In fact most students fall very close to completely satisfied with a 6 or 7 on the 7-point scale. Respondents to the Monitoring the Future study are grouped on the right indicating that the vast majority of students are satisfied with their personal safety. Is this an interesting result from the study? Does it fit with what you may have heard on TV or from a newspaper about safety in high schools?

You will study three measures of central tendency: mode, median, and mean. Your text shows that the level of measurement is one criterion for selecting a measure of central tendency. This Chapter demonstrates a second criterion – skew – which, when present, biases the mean so that it is no longer useful as a measure of central tendency. If a distribution is skewed, you should select the median as the best statistic for describing the average.

The mean is sensitive to extreme scores. The mean will be pulled to the side where the extreme scores are located. In a left-tail skew the value of the mean will be less than the median. In a right-tail distribution the mean will be greater than the median. In a symmetric or normal distribution they have the same value.

DATA ANALYSIS EXAMPLE USING FOX'S CALCULATOR

Research problem:

Truancy is a problem in many urban school systems. A researcher gathers data for a random sample of twenty students in a middle school. The raw data on unexcused absences where a child missed school without a legitimate reason (e.g. sickness) are as follows:

0, 0, 1, 1, 0, 0, 1, 2, 0, 19, 0, 0, 1, 1, 10, 2, 0, 0, 1, 2

Enter these twenty cases into the FREQUENCY DISTRIBUTIONS option in Fox's Statistics calculator. The results are shown on the following page.

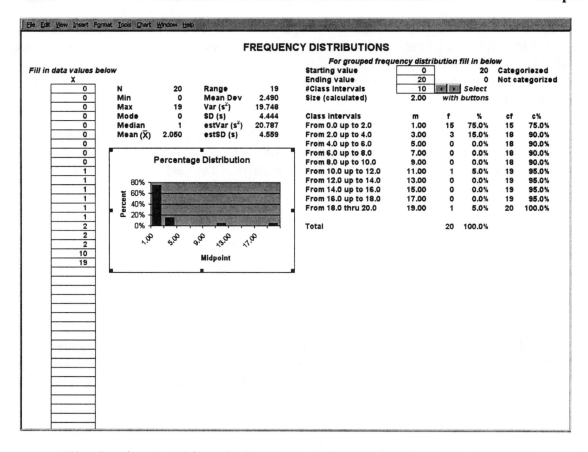

The data is entered into the box on the left. I sorted the values from highest to lowest prior to typing in the values. You can do this or just enter them from the list. In order to get a histogram, you have to enter a starting and ending value, and the number of class intervals. I entered 0 as the starting (or minimum) value and 20 as the ending (or maximum) value. I chose 10 as the number of class intervals. This is the number of bars that will be shown in the percentage distribution.

Look back at the figure on skewness (on page 63) and compare it to the percentage distribution above. What does it look like? My guess is that it is skewed to the right so that we will expect a mean that is larger than the median. Is this correct? The statistics are calculated as a mean of 2.05 and a median of 1. The mean is larger than the median. Where is the mode? It is at 0. The median falls between the mean and the mode. It does appear that we have a positively skewed distribution. Most students have zero unexcused absences (mode=0). The average number of unexcused absences is one class (Median = 1). The mean is probably not a good measure of central tendency in this case because of extreme scores. One student had 19 unexcused absences.

Fox's calculator is very useful when you have a small number of cases to analyze. SPSS is a more powerful tool when you wish to work with large data files. It also calculates a statistic that estimates the degree of skewness.

DATA ANALYSIS EXAMPLE USING SPSS

Research Problem: How much television does the average American watch per day? We can answer this question by using information from the General Social Survey looking at hours per day of t.v. (TVHOURS). We will determine whether the mean or the median a better estimate of the central tendency of this distribution.

We will obtain a skewness statistic to assess whether or not the distribution can be considered as "normal." If the ratio of skewness statistic to its standard error is **greater that 2.0 in magnitude**, we will say that the distribution is skewed and that the mean is no longer an appropriate measure of central tendency. If this happens, we rely upon the median as our best estimate of the average. If this ratio of skewness to standard error is **less than 2.0 in magnitude**, we will say that the distribution is symmetric and that the mean is the most appropriate measure of central tendency. Interpreting the skewness statistic is a bit more complicated as it is also sensitive to sample size. For very large samples, over 2000 cases, just look to see whether the skewness statistic itself is over 2 in magnitude.

Histograms in SPSS: Histograms provide a pictorial representation of frequency distributions. The computer program will modify the class intervals so that they fit on a single page. The length of the bar represents the frequency of occurrence for a class interval. The length of bars are approximate. The class intervals are bounded by the smallest valid number (left-end) and the largest valid number. The middle value of an interval is the mid-point of a class interval. For each histogram, note the definition of the interval width. It doesn't have to be one unit.

Computer output: The following histogram shows the distribution for "hours per day watching television." Find TVHOURS in the codebook for the General Social Survey.

The histogram shows several things. First, the mode is located by finding the longest bar in the histogram. It is a score of "1." Reading the codebook, we see that the modal category (mode) is one hour of television. We need to read the codebook to identify what numbers mean because a 1 isn't always 1 of something. For example, look at RINCOM98 in the codebook and you'll see that 1 isn't 1 dollar. In this example, "1" is one hour of watching television. The frequency in the histogram is equivalent to the valid frequency that is reported in a frequency distribution. We see that the mode is somewhere close to 120 of 466 respondents. The 466 is shown as the N at the bottom right of the histogram.

Next, we will make a guess as to the shape of the distribution. Quite clearly this doesn't look like a perfect bell shape or normal distribution. There are many more cases on the left and it looks like far fewer cases on the right side. In order to guess whether the mean or the median will be larger, I suspect that there is a positive skew; it looks like some Americans watch a great deal of television and these cases will skew the mean to the right. Therefore, my guess is that the mean will be larger than the median because of the apparently right tail. Keep in mind that this is just a guess. We will calculate a skewness statistic and standard error of skewness to see whether our guess was accurate in order to make a decision about whether the mean or the median is a better measure of the average for the variable.

Histogram

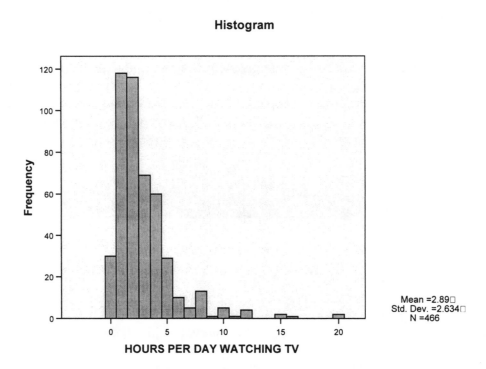

Computer work: We will use a statistical test to assess our guess about skewness and the placement of the mean and median. The criterion for a significant difference is that skewness is greater than 2.0 to indicate a significant difference between the mean and median. We use the FREQUENCIES procedure, as in Chapter 1, select statistics, and then check the appropriate boxes to obtain statistics. Below you can see that the mean, median, and skewness are checked. Click on "Continue" to move back to the main dialogue box in FREQUENCIES and then click OK.

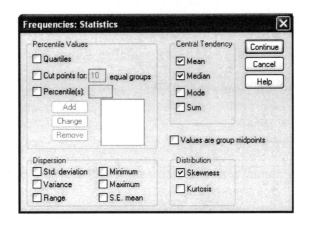

The results of the statistical analysis are shown in the table. The valid N is 466. This N is less than 2000 which means we will evaluate skewness by comparing it to its standard error. (If the N was larger than 2000, we would just read the Sk=2.667 directly and say it is significantly skewed.)

Statistics

TVHOURS HOURS PER DAY WATCHING TV

N	Valid	466
	Missing	1034
Mean		2.89
Median		2.00
Skewness		2.667
Std. Error of Skewness		.113

The ratio of skewness to its standard error is +2.667 / .113 = +23.6. The ratio is larger in magnitude than 2.0 which suggests that this distribution is positively skewed. This result indicates that the mean may be a biased statistic and that the distribution may not be normal. Our criterion was that it had to be above 2 in magnitude in order for us to say that the distribution was skewed. It is above 2. Thus, we say that the mean is biased and that the median is a more appropriate measure of central tendency for this distribution. We conclude that the median value of 2 represents the television viewing habits of a typical American. It is important to take all of these statistics and to provide an overall summary of results.

Interpretation: An analysis of the distribution in television viewing habits of Americans was conducted using information from the 2004 General Social Survey. Television viewing was evaluated by asking Americans the number of hours per day that they watched television. This variable was operationalized hours per day where "0" means none to a theoretical "24" hours. For this variable, the best indicator of the average is the median because the distribution is highly skewed to the right. The ratio of the skew to its standard error is 23.6. The positive value for this ratio indicates a right skew suggesting some persons watch a very great number of hours of television. The median score is a 2 which indicates that a typical American watches two hours of television per day.

Note that an interpretation should describe:

- The source of information
- The scale (in this case a question on a survey)
- The analysis (in this case an assessment of skewness)
- The decision (that the median is the best measure of central tendency for this variable)
- And an interpretation of the best measure of central tendency (the median for this example).

KEY TERMS

Bias	Histogram
Central Tendency	Normal distribution
Mean	Ratio of Skewness to its standard error
Median	Skewness
Mode	Standard error of skewness

CHAPTER 3 PROBLEMS

Calculate the mode, median and mean for each variable. Use the percentage distribution or histograms for each variable to estimate whether there is a significant skew in the distributions.

Tasks:
1. For each of the variables, identify the level of measurement.
2. Use the histograms to find the mode. Make your guess about skewness and estimate where the mean will fall in relation to the median.
3. Use the computer to find the mean, median, and skewness.
4. For each variable, write a short summary of two or three sentences. You should describe the skew of the distribution and indicate which measure of central tendency is best for the distribution.

Name _____   **Date** _____

1.   Use Fox's Statistics Calculator to analyze the following data.

A researcher examines court dispositions on sentencing where different judges make sentencing recommendations for very similar convictions.   Twenty cases were identified and sentence length in years is shown below:

1, 3, 3, 4, 4, 5, 5, 6, 6, 7, 7, 7, 8, 9, 10, 10, 10, 11, 12, 18

For the percentage distribution, use a starting value of 0, an ending value of 20 and number of intervals of 5.

What is the level of measurement?

Draw the percentage distribution below (roughly)

From the percentage distribution, where do you think the mean falls?

Is the mean or median bigger? (circle guess)

Name _____   **Date** _____

From the Statistics Calculator:

Mean _____

Median _____

Mode _____

Which measure is best: Mean / Median (Circle)

Interpretation of results:

Going beyond the output: Using your college library, find a research article on "sentencing disparity." Write a short essay on why this issue is important to study.

Name _____   **Date** _____

2.   From the General Social Survey, political views (POLVIEWS)

Use the codebook to complete the following:

Variable name

Level of Measurement

Guess: Mean or median is bigger (circle guess)

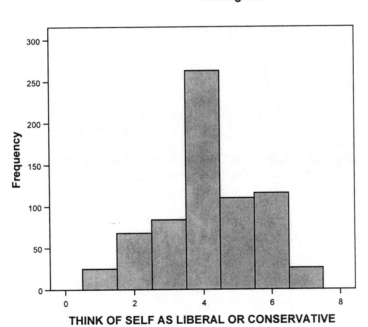

Histogram

Mean =4.18
Std. Dev. =1.406
N =692

THINK OF SELF AS LIBERAL OR CONSERVATIVE

What is the mode?   _____

Name _____   **Date** _____

Use the computer to calculate:

Mean _____

Median _____

Skewness _____

Which measure is best: Mean / Median (Circle)

Interpretation of results:

Going beyond the output: Use your college library to find an article on political views. Write a short essay on your findings.

Name _____   Date _____

3.   From the General Social Survey, analyze how often people in America pray (PRAY).

Use the codebook to complete the following:

Variable name

Level of Measurement

Histogram

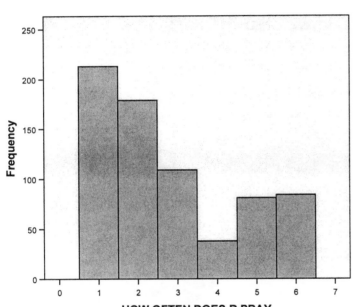

Mean =2.78☐
Std. Dev. =1.735☐
N =704

Guess: Mean or median is bigger (circle)

What is the mode?

Name _____   **Date** _____

Use the computer to calculate:

Mean _____

Median _____

Skewness _____

Which measure is best: Mean / Median (Circle)

Interpretation of results:

Going beyond the output: Find an article on "religiosity." Why is this an important issue for people's quality of life?

Name _____   **Date** _____

4. From the General Social Survey, analyze the distribution of family's income in 2004 (income98).

Use the codebook to complete the following:

Variable name

Level of Measurement

Guess: Mean or median is bigger (circle)

Histogram

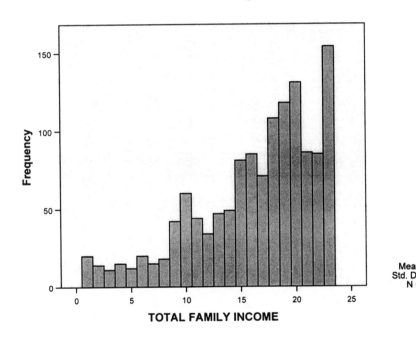

Mean =16.32▫
Std. Dev. =5.502▫
N =1,320

What is the mode?

Name _____   **Date** _____

Use the computer to calculate:

Mean _____

Median _____

Skewness _____

Which measure is best: Mean / Median (Circle)

Interpretation of results:

Going beyond the output: Find an article on "income inequality."
Write a short essay on the distribution of income in America.

Name _____   Date _____

5.   From the Monitoring the Future study, satisfaction with own friends (V1646).

Use the codebook to complete the following:

Variable name

Level of Measurement

Guess: Mean or median is bigger (circle)

Histogram

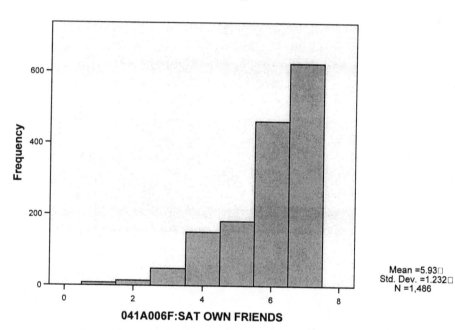

Mean =5.93
Std. Dev. =1.232
N =1,486

What is the mode?

Name _____   **Date** _____

Computer calculations of:

Mean _____

Median _____

Skewness _____

Which measure is best: Mean / Median (Circle)

Interpretation of results:

Going beyond the output: Use your college library, find an article on the importance of "friendship." Compare the results from your analysis of the 2004 Monitoring the Future study to the article.

VARIABILITY: SKEWNESS AND KURTOSIS

INTRODUCTION

In Chapter 5 we will look in great detail at the standard deviation using z-scores to assess whether a distribution is a "normal" distribution. In most instances though you're going to want to know how to quickly assess the shape of a distribution and then move to interpret the appropriate statistics: mean (or median) and standard deviation (or range). In this chapter you will:

1.   look at skewness and kurtosis; and
2.   choose appropriate statistics.

Measures of distribution

The figure below shows a symmetric (normal) distribution, a positive (or right-tailed) skew, and a negative (or left-tailed) skew. We used the skewness statistic in Chapter 5 to determine whether or not the mean or median was the most appropriate measure of central tendency. If skewness is over 2 in magnitude the mean and standard deviation are biased and we use the median and range as measures of central tendency and dispersion.

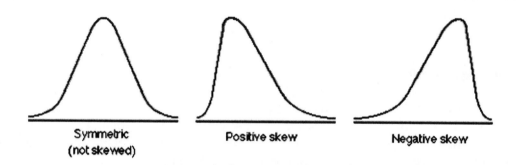

| Symmetric (not skewed) | Positive skew | Negative skew |

Figure 1   Skewness

A second measure of symmetry is kurtosis. The figure shows that distributions can be peaked (leptokurtic) or flat (platykurtic). An Australian named these terms as lepto (+ values) after two kangaroos lepping, and platy (- values) after the Australian platypus. He called the symmetric (normal curve) a mesokurtic distribution with a kurtosis of zero (0).

81

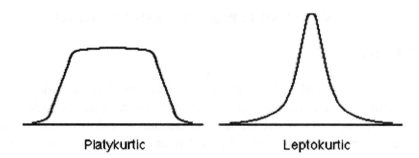

Platykurtic   Leptokurtic

Figure 2 Kurtosis

Looking at the platykurtic distribution, the scores may fall a large distance from the mean and we would expect a larger standard deviation. With a leptokurtic distribution, the scores fall close to the mean and we'd have a relatively small standard deviation.

If you were to take an exam, what kind of skewness and kurtosis would you like to have? I think I'd like one with a negative skew and leptokurtosis. That is, the exam would have high scores and most people would score close to the high average. Compare this to a positive skew and leptokurtosis and you'd find a low average and most people scored close to it.

Similar to chapter 3, we will calculate a ratio by dividing the kurtosis by its standard error. If the ratio of kurtosis to the standard error of kurtosis is greater in magnitude that 2.0 then we will conclude that the kurtosis is significant.

Choosing appropriate statistics

If the distribution of a variable turns out to be normal, then the mean and standard deviation are the appropriate statistics. If a distribution is not normal, the median and range will be recommended as the most appropriate measures of central tendency and dispersion. These tests for skewness and kurtosis are important tests for helping us to see the shape of the distribution of a variable and for helping us to understand whether they may be any problems using the mean and standard deviation in more advanced statistical procedures.

DATA ANALYSIS EXAMPLE

Research problem: Describe the distribution of students' political beliefs (V167).

Codebook information: Use the codebook to get the basic information about the scale. Note that the scale is a Likert scale which ranges from 1 "Very conservative" to 6 "Radical." For purposes of our analysis we will treat this variable as if it is an interval level variable so that we can calculate a mean and standard deviation.

Computer analysis: Use the FREQUENCIES procedure to calculate measures of central tendency, dispersion, and distribution. Click the boxes as shown below.

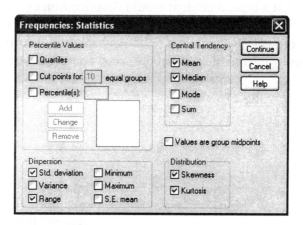

Results: Looking first at skewness, we find sk=.239 with a standard error of .079 yielding a ratio of 3.03. This ratio indicates the distribution is skewed substantially to the right. Considering kurtosis, the ku=.016 with a standard error of .159 yielding a ratio of .10 is a small positive value or a mesokurtic distribution. Thus, we would describe the distribution of political beliefs of students as having an asymmetric distribution (positive skew and no kurtosis). Since the distribution fails the skewness test, we will recommend a median and range as appropriate statistics.

Statistics

v167 042C12 :R'POL BLF RADCL

N	Valid	950
	Missing	550
Mean		3.16
Median		3.00
Std. Deviation		1.162
Skewness		.239
Std. Error of Skewness		.079
Kurtosis		.016
Std. Error of Kurtosis		.159
Range		5

Summary interpretation: We used survey data from the Monitoring the Future Study (2004) to assess the distribution of students' political beliefs. The question used a Likert scale varying from very conservative to radical beliefs. We found a positively skewed distribution (ratio of skewness = 3.0). A positive skew indicates that high scores where students said they had radical beliefs were extreme scores. Considering kurtosis, this variable is a seemingly mesokurtic distribution or relatively normal distribution (ratio of kurtosis =0.1).

We have found a non-normal or asymmetric distribution because this distribution is positively skewed. Hence, the median value is a more appropriate measure of the "average." The survey suggests that a typical student would describe him or herself as having moderate political beliefs (Md=3). The range in political beliefs of high school students spans from very conservative to very radical. Nonetheless, in this mesokurtic distribution we suggest that most American High School students in 2004 fell between conservative and liberal in their political views.

Key terms

Kurtosis
>Leptokurtic
>Mesokurtic
>Platykurtic

Skewness
>Postive/right-tail skew
>None/ normal distribution
>Negative/ left-tail skew

Name _____   **Date** _____

1.   Use the Monitoring the Future study to examine the dispersion of the number of traffic tickets (V197).

Codebook information (variable name, min, max, level of measurement, etc.)

Descriptive statistics

Mean = _____   Median = _____

Skewness = _____   Kurtosis = _____

Standard error of sk= _____   Standard error of Ku = _____

Ratio of sk/se= _____   Ratio of Ku / se = _____

Standard deviation = _____   Range = _____

Draw a picture of the distribution

Interpretation of results:

Name _____   **Date** _____

2.   Use the Monitoring the Future study to examine the dispersion of satisfaction with life as a whole (V1652).

Codebook information (variable name, min, max, level of measurement, etc.)

Descriptive statistics

Mean = _____   Median = _____

Skewness = _____   Kurtosis = _____

Standard error of sk= _____   Standard error of Ku = _____

Ratio of sk/se= _____   Ratio of Ku / se = _____

Standard deviation = _____   Range = _____

Draw a picture of the distribution

Interpretation of results:

Name _____   **Date** _____

3.   Use the General Social Survey to examine the dispersion of in socioeconomic status (SEI).

Codebook information (variable name, min, max, level of measurement, etc.)

Descriptive statistics

Mean = _____   Median = _____

Skewness = _____   Kurtosis = _____

Standard error of sk= _____   Standard error of Ku = _____

Ratio of sk/se= _____   Ratio of Ku / se = _____

Standard deviation = _____   Range = _____

Draw a picture of the distribution

Interpretation of results:

Name _____   **Date** _____

4.   Use the General Social Survey to examine a variable of your choice. It should be an interval level variable (or one where you can make this assumption).

Codebook information (variable name, min, max, level of measurement, etc.)

Descriptive statistics

Mean = _____   Median = _____

Skewness = _____   Kurtosis = _____

Standard error of sk= _____   Standard error of Ku = _____

Ratio of sk/se= _____   Ratio of Ku / se = _____

Standard deviation = _____   Range = _____

Draw a picture of the distribution

Interpretation of results:

Z-SCORES AND THE NORMAL CURVE

INTRODUCTION

This chapter introduces properties of the normal curve and uses the standard deviation to critically assess whether a distribution is a "normal" distribution. If it is not, there are substantial implications about whether the mean and standard deviation are appropriate statistics. You will:

1.   look at measures of variability;
2.   use the mean and standard deviation to compute z-scores; and
3.   compare the observed (empirical) distribution of variables to a normal distribution.

Measures of Variability

Measures of variability describe the amount of dispersion in a variable. Selecting a measure depends on the level of analysis of a variable. The range (R) is a simple measure of variability, applicable for ordinal variables and higher, where you take the difference between the smallest (minimum) and largest (maximum) score. The variance (s^2) and standard deviation (s), applicable to interval and ratio level variables, are the most commonly used measures of variation. The variance is a measure that looks at how far each score is above or below the mean score in a distribution, and it takes into account how many cases are in the population. We will generate these statistics from the sample and make inferences about the population parameters.

The mean and the standard deviation are two of the basic building blocks which form the foundation of most elementary and advanced statistics. A key assumption for many of the statistics that we will use in later chapters in this workbook is that a variable is normally distributed. This chapter provides a method to test this assumption whereby we can describe with great precision the dispersion in a variable.

Ultimately, while we are working with sample statistics for the mean ($\bar{x}$) and standard deviation (s) we are doing this to estimate the true population parameters of the mean (μ) and standard deviation (σ) of a population. Consider the Monitoring the Future Study which examines a sample of high school seniors yet we wish to generalize to all high school seniors in the United States. And, when using the General Social Survey with a sample of American adults we wish to generalize to all American adults.

Z-scores

In order to conduct our test, we will need to convert the scores on a variable into a standard score or z-score. A z-score is a standardized score showing the difference between a particular score (x) and the population mean (μ) taking into account the standard deviation of the variable (σ).

The z-score shows, in standard units, where a case falls in a normal distribution.

$$z = (x-\mu) / \sigma$$

You may convert raw scores to standard scores; or you may convert z-scores into raw scores.

$$x = \mu + z (\sigma).$$

Normal distribution

The standard normal distribution (bell curve) is symmetric with a mean of zero and a standard deviation of 1. We know the theoretical area under the curve for any specified z-score. Using Appendix C in Levin and Fox, the z-score table shows that there is 34.13% of the area under the curve as we go from the mean (0) to one standard deviation above the mean (1). Figure 1 below shows a graphical presentation of this area. How much area is there between 0 and –1? It's the same distance as from 0 to +1. Thus, the answer is also 34.13. Find the area in the Appendix going from 0 to +2 standard deviations. And, from 0 to +3 standard deviations. The answers are 47.72% and 49.84%.

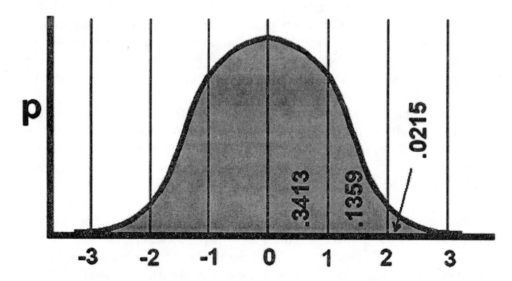

Figure 1. The percent of total area under the normal curve

To complete a "strong test" of the fit of a variable empirical distribution with the normal curve we would like to examine every 1 unit area under the curve: 0-1; 1-2; and 2-3 on both sides of the curve. From the normal curve, we know the theoretical distribution of cases. We will use the actual mean and standard deviation to calculate the expected distribution for a variable and compare the observed values to expected values.

The vast majority of z-scores usually fall within three standard deviations of the mean.

Thus, we will limit our test for all practical purposes to scores that fall within –3 to + 3 standard deviations from the mean.

The area under the bell curve is used to make statements about probability of occurrence of the distribution of cases. Researchers typically are interested in how many cases fall within 1, 2, and 3 standard deviations of the mean as 34.1%; 13.6%, and 2.1%. To complete our test, we will use a criterion of + or – 5% on the difference between the observed and theoretical percentages in each interval. If we find that all intervals fit this criterion, we will say that we have a strong fit to the normal distribution. If any of the intervals fail to meet this criterion, we do not have a strong fit.

In many instances a variable may be close to normal where most cases are near the center of the distribution but with a slight skew to one side. We can relax our assessment by adjusting our test to see whether cases fall within –1 to +1 standard deviations; -2 to 2; and –3 to 3. Figure 2 shows the approximate areas under the curve in these intervals. If our test using a criterion of + or – 5% shows a fit to the distribution, we will call this a weak fit to the normal distribution. In fact, in many instances this is what we are going to find.

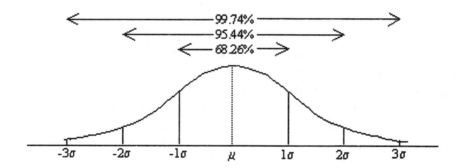

Figure 2. The percent of total area for the weak fit to the normal curve

The z-scores in a normal distribution are "theoretical." The degree to which these characteristics are found for a variable depends on the "observed" distribution of the variable. A variable which is skewed may only approximate a few of the characteristics of a normal distribution. A variable which is highly skewed may not have any of these characteristics.

When we complete the exercises for this chapter we will use a table as shown on the following page to make our assessment of fit.

z-score	-3 to -2	-2 to –1	-1 to 0	0 to 1	1 to 2	2 to 3
Strong fit	2.1%	13.6%	34.1%	34.1%	13.6%	2.1%
Weak fit for total areas			68%			
		95%				
	99.74%					

For example, we expect about 34.1 % of cases to fall within 1 standard deviation above the mean. The table below shows the approximate number of cases under the curve for each interval.

DATA ANALYSIS EXAMPLE

Research problem: What is the distribution of high school students' satisfaction with their own friends? A recent study in the American Sociological Review by McPherson, Smith-Lovin and Brashears (2006) talks about how friendship networks of American adults have changed over the past twenty years. Could it be that people don't value friends as much? Think about it for a moment. How satisfied are you with your own friendships? And, what do you think the average American senior in high school would say about his or her friendships? Draw out a rough picture for yourself with the scale ranging from completely satisfied (7) to completely dissatisfied (1). We will use the Monitoring the Future Study to compare the actual distribution of satisfaction with friends to the normal curve. We will assess whether there is a strong or a weak fit of the observed distribution compared to theoretical expectations for a normal curve.

Codebook information: Use the codebook to get the basic information on level of measurement.

Codebook information		Statistics	
Variable name	V1646	Mean	
Variable label	Satisfaction with friendships	SD	

Minimum	1 "Completely dissatisfied"	Variance	
Maximum	7 "Completely satisfied"	Range	
Metric	1 unit of satisfaction	Valid cases	
Level of Measurement	Interval / scale		

Use the computer to obtain *descriptive statistics*: In order to calculate the z-scores we are going to need a mean and standard deviation. We can obtain the range and variance at the same time. Click on Analyze, Descriptive Statistics, and then descriptives. Click in the box on the bottom

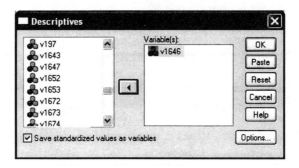

left to save standardized values as variables. This will create a new variable ZV1646 which is V11646 turned into z-scores. You'll also need to click on options to select the Range and variance.

As you complete the exercise, write the mean, standard deviation, range and variance into the earlier table. The SPSS output from the DESCRIPTIVES procedure is show below:

Descriptive Statistics

	N	Range	Minimum	Maximum	Mean	Std. Deviation	Variance
v1646 041A006F:SAT OWN FRIENDS	1486	6	1	7	5.93	1.232	1.518
Valid N (listwise)	1486						

We're going to use the mean and standard deviation to calculate the continuous and discrete raw scores that would be expected if the observed variable is truly a normal distribution. This is the formula: $x = \mu + z(\sigma)$ where we will insert the mean and standard deviation to calculate the lower interval for the continuous raw score.

For example, at –4 standard deviations $x = 5.93 + -4(1.23)$; $x = 1.01$. Write this number into the column for the lower bound of the continuous raw score for –4. Find 1.01 in the Table on the next page. Calculate the lower limit for –3. That is $x = 5.93 + -3(1.23) = 2.24$. Repeat these calculations for all of the lower limits. The solutions are shown in the Table.

What is the expected value at 0 standard deviations from the mean? The answer is the mean. Since we know this value must be the mean, use it as a back-up check on your calculations.

Next, we will estimate the upper limit as the next number between the upper limit and the lower limit for the adjacent interval. For example, if the lower limit for –3 to –2 is 2.24 then the next smallest number is 2.23. Do this for all of the intervals except the last one. You can estimate it if you calculate another z-score for +5 on the lower limit or you can just say it is expected to be any z-score higher than 9.62.

Class intervals						Distribution	
Continuous z-score		Continuous raw Score		Discrete raw Score		% of cases per interval	
Lower	Upper	Lower	Upper	Lower	Upper	Observed	Expected
-4	-3	1.01	2.23				
-3	-2	2.24	3.46				
-2	-1	3.47	4.69				
-1	0	4.70	5.92				
0	1	5.93	7.15				
1	2	7.16	8.36				
2	3	8.39	9.61				
3	4	9.62	Higher				

Next, we're going to want to determine the theoretical values for discrete scores in each interval. This is easy! Just look to see the smallest whole number in an interval and the largest whole number in an interval. Of course, we only want to work with numbers that were on our original survey question. Recall that it went from 1 (Completely dissatisfied) to 7 (Completely satisfied). Thus, we need to find out where scores of 1 to 7 fall in the theoretical normal distribution. When expected values come up as a number that falls outside the possible numbers on our scale then we will note these as not applicable (NA).

Where does "1" go? Can it go between 1.01 and 2.23? No. 1.01 is bigger than 1.00. The "1" would fall in the next lowest distribution -5 to -4 which is goes beyond our chart. What whole numbers can fit between 1.01 and 2.23? Starting with the lower boundary, what is the smallest whole number that fits between 1.01 and 2.23? The answer is "2" is the smallest whole number in this interval. What is the largest number? Can 3 fit here? No, it is too big. Move to the next interval between 2.24 and 3.46. Does "2" fit here as the lower boundary? No, 2 is too small to fit between 2.24 and 3.46. How about 3? Yes, 3 fits between 2.24 and 3.46 as our lower limit. It is also the biggest whole number that fits in this interval.

For the next interval, 3.47 to 4.69, what values fit here? How about 3? No, it is too small (and we've already located where it goes). The answers are 4 is the lower limit and 4 is the upper limit. The completed table is shown on the following page. Not applicable (n.a.) is noted in intervals where no values are possible. These discrete values represent the scores for satisfaction with friends if the actual distribution conforms to what is expected in a normal distribution.

We're ready to complete the table by obtaining a frequency distribution for the variable. We know the expected distribution as the area that falls under the normal curve. We will complete the table by generating a frequency distribution to find the observed frequencies. Wow. Are you overwhelmed yet? We're almost there.

v1646 041A006F:SAT OWN FRIENDS

		Frequency	Percent	Valid Percent	Cumulative Percent
Valid	1 COMP DIS:(1)	8	.5	.5	.5
	2	14	.9	.9	1.5
	3	48	3.2	3.2	4.7
	4 NEUTRAL:(4)	150	10.0	10.1	14.8
	5	181	12.1	12.2	27.0
	6	461	30.7	31.0	58.0
	7 COMP SAT:(7)	624	41.6	42.0	100.0
	Total	1486	99.1	100.0	
Missing	-9 MISSING	14	.9		
Total		1500	100.0		

Class intervals						Distribution	
Continuous z-score		Continuous raw Score		Discrete raw Score		% of cases per interval	
Lower	Upper	Lower	Upper	Lower	Upper	Observed	Expected
-4	-3	1.01	2.23	2	2	0.9	0
-3	-2	2.24	3.46	3	3	3.2	2.1
-2	-1	3.47	4.69	4	4	10.1	13.6
-1	0	4.70	5.92	5	5	12.2	34.1
0	1	5.93	7.15	6	7	73.0	34.1
1	2	7.16	8.36	n.a.	n.a.	0.0	13.6
2	3	8.39	9.61	n.a.	n.a.	0.0	2.1
3	4	9.62	Higher	n.a.	n.a.	0.0	0

How many not applicable (n.a.) raw scores do you see if the frequency distribution? That is, scores that fall outside 1 to 9? The answer is 0. Write 0.0 in for each of the n.a.'s. What percentage of satisfaction is observed for scores of 2? Find the valid percentages for 2 which is 0.9 percent. Write this percentage into the interval. What percentage of scores are 3? It is 3.2 percent. Continue adding up the percentages for each intervals. Notice for discrete scores 6 and 7 you will add their valid percentages (31.0+42.0=73.0) because 6 and 7 fall in this interval. When you are finished, add up all of the subtotals for observed percentages to see that you get 100.0 or something within rounding error. The total for this table is 99.4 which shows that we have added numbers correctly in the frequency table. If you're out by more than 1 percent, you should probably recheck your work to make sure that you added up all of the possible categories. In our case, the missing amount is the scores for "1" which falls outside the range of our chart. Now that the information is shown in the chart, we finally are ready to assess the fit of the observed distribution to the normal curve.

Assessing fit: We will always use a criterion of five percent to decide whether or not there is a difference in the percentage of cases in the observed versus the normal distribution. Simply subtract the observed percentage from the expected percentage for each interval to see whether the difference is more than 5 percent (lower or higher). In this example, the distribution clearly fails to fit the strong version of the empirical distribution. There are instances where it fits (e.g.

96

0.9-0=0.9 which is with 5 percent). However, there are several instances larger (or smaller) than would be expected (e.g. 12.2-34.1=-21.9; 73.0–34.1 = 38.9 neither of which is within 5 percent). We only need one failure in order to say that the distribution does not fit the strong test of whether it is a normal distribution.

A distribution that fits the strong version will always fit the weak version of the empirical distribution. If the strong version fails, we should see if there is a weak fit to the normal curve? We will test the weak fit below to illustrate the calculations to add up the cases between each of the intervals.

In this example, which cases fall between –1 as a lower limit and +1 as an upper limit? That is, which raw scores are expected to fall between –1 and + 1 standard deviations? The answer is discrete scores of 5 through 7. What percentage of observed cases fell in this interval? Add up the following: 12.2+31.0+42.0 = 85.5.

Comparison for weak Distribution	% Observed	% Expected
+/- 1 SD	85.2	68
+/- 2 SD	95.3	95
+/- 3 SD	98.5	99.75%

Do the same calculations for scores between –2 and +2 and –3 and +3 standard deviations. The solutions are shown in the Table above. We again use a criterion of +/- 5 percent to assess the fit of the weak version of the empirical distribution subtracting the observed from the expected percentage of cases. In the first interval, subtract 85.2-68.0 to obtain 17.2. This result clearly fails to meet our criterion of within 5 percent. While the remaining intervals are within 5 percent, it only takes one failure for us to say that this distribution fails to fit the weak version of the empirical distribution.

If there were no differences of +/- 5 percent in any of the intervals we would say that the test of fit had succeeded. In this example, we found a failure of fit for the strong version of the empirical distribution and a failure of fit for the weak version of the empirical distribution. The importance of this finding is that the distribution of the variable is NOT normally distributed so that we will strongly advise against using the mean and standard deviation are not appropriate statistics for this variable. We've done a very rigorous test to determine whether we should be using a mean and standard deviation with this variable.

In your statistics course you will see that the mean and standard deviation are the foundation for most sophisticated statistical tests. When a variable fails to fit the strong version of the empirical distribution then it may not be appropriate to use sophisticated statistical tests. When a variable has a weak fit we will usually continue to use these more advanced statistics but provide a qualifier about our results that the distribution has only a weak fit to the test for a normal distribution. If a statistical test assumes a normal distribution, you can test this using the methods outlined in this chapter.

It is important in any data analysis that you go beyond the computer output. You should summarize the information so that a reader can understand the basic information you wish to present. Telling someone about a z-score of 1.0 is not all that meaningful. You should refer back to an original metric (if there is one).

Interpretation: We conducted a test to assess the distribution of American high school students' satisfaction with their friends using data from the Monitoring the Future study. We compared the actual percentages of cases to a normal distribution and found that students' satisfaction with their friends fails to fit the strong or weak versions of the empirical distribution. This test assesses whether a variable is normally distributed. We conclude that it is not appropriate to use a mean or a standard deviation in future analysis of this variable. We conclude that this variable is not normally distributed. Close analysis of this distribution shows that most high school seniors are highly satisfied with their friendships.

We're done! We've done an incredible amount of work in order to assess whether the mean and standard deviation are appropriate statistics. If there is a strong fit, they clearly apply. If there is a weak fit, they probably can still be used but the researcher should explain to the reader that there may be problems. If the distribution does not fit, then the mean and standard deviation should not be used and the analyst should recommend that the median and range be used. This is a time consuming test, but it is important that a researcher know the properties of data that he or she is using in more complex tests.

Note that we can obtain the same information by examining the frequency distribution of the transformed variable that we calculated when we checked the box to save standardized values as variables in the "DESCRIPTIVES" procedure. It's frequency distribution is shown below. The raw "1" translates into a z-score of -4.00484. We could use this table looking for values between -4 and -3 with 0.9; -3 to -2 at 3.2 percent; and continue on down until we had identified the observed percentages within each interval of the continuous z score.

Zv1646 Zscore: 041A006F:SAT OWN FRIENDS

		Frequency	Percent	Valid Percent	Cumulative Percent
Valid	-4.00484	8	.5	.5	.5
	-3.19327	14	.9	.9	1.5
	-2.38171	48	3.2	3.2	4.7
	-1.57015	150	10.0	10.1	14.8
	-.75859	181	12.1	12.2	27.0
	.05298	461	30.7	31.0	58.0
	.86454	624	41.6	42.0	100.0
	Total	1486	99.1	100.0	
Missing	System	14	.9		
Total		1500	100.0		

Either method using the raw scores or the z scores will allow a test of the fit of the distribution to the normal curve. Calculation of the continuous and discrete raw scores though should give you a greater appreciation on how to convert standard to raw scores and vice versa.

KEY TERMS

Descriptives
Normal curve
Standard deviation
Strong fit
Weak fit
Z-score

CHAPTER 5 PROBLEMS

Research Problems: Summarize the statistical variation of the following variables from the General Social Survey, 2004:

1.   Evenings out at bar. (SOCBAR)
2.   Evenings out with friends (SOCFRND)

Descriptive Statistics

	N	Mean	Std. Deviation
SOCBAR SPEND EVENING AT BAR	469	5.61	1.702
SOCFREND SPEND EVENING WITH FRIENDS	469	3.89	1.597
Valid N (listwise)	468		

Using the Monitoring the Future Study, summarize:

3.   Ease of getting cocaine (V1782)
4.   A variable of your choice
       You will have to generate the descriptive statistics for variables from MTF.

Tasks:
1. Use the codebook to identify the characteristics of variables (assume that ordinal variables are at the interval level). Copy the information for each variable on to worksheets; each worksheet is for one variable.
2. The means and standard deviations for Rincom98 and Sexfreq are provided above. Use this information to calculate the continuous and discrete raw scores prior to coming into the computer lab.
3. Use the descriptives procedure in SPSS for windows to get the remaining statistics for SOCBAR and SOCFREND and all of the statistics for variables from the Monitoring the Future study (mean, standard deviation, variance, range, and valid cases). Write the statistics on to the worksheets.
4. Use SPSS for windows to obtain a frequency distribution for each variable. Copy the information from each z-score distribution to the worksheets.
5. Calculate the continuous and discrete class intervals for each variable. Compare the observed (empirical) distributions with the normal distribution.

Interpretations: For each variable, write a short summary of the variable using the mean, standard deviation and range of scores. Also, report on an aspect of the strong (or weak) fit to the normal distribution.

Name _____   **Date** _____

1. Determine the fit to the normal curve for "Nights out at the bar in 2004." (SOCBAR) Use the worksheet on the following page to make your assessment.

Comparison for weak Distribution	% Observed	% Expected
+/- 1 SD		68
+/- 2 SD		95
+/- 3 SD		99.75%

Interpretation of results:

Codebook information		Statistics	
Variable name		Mean	
Variable label		SD	
Minimum		Variance	
Maximum		Range	
Metric		Valid cases	
Level of Measurement			

Class intervals						Distribution	
Continuous z-score		Continuous raw score		Discrete raw score		% of cases per interval	
Lower	Upper	Lower	Upper	Lower	Upper	Observed	Expected
-4	-3						0
-3	-2						2.1
-2	-1						13.6
-1	0						34.1
0	1						34.1
1	2						13.6
2	3						2.1
3	4						0

Name _____   Date _____

2.   Determine the fit to the normal curve for "How often spend nights out with friends (SOCFREND)" Use the worksheet on the following page to make your assessment.

Comparison for weak Distribution	% Observed	% Expected
+/- 1 SD		68
+/- 2 SD		95
+/- 3 SD		99.75%

Interpretation of results:

Codebook information		Statistics	
Variable name		Mean	
Variable label		SD	
Minimum		Variance	
Maximum		Range	
Metric		Valid cases	
Level of Measurement			

Class intervals						Distribution	
Continuous z-score		Continuous raw score		Discrete raw score		% of cases per interval	
Lower	Upper	Lower	Upper	Lower	Upper	Observed	Expected
-4	-3						0
-3	-2						2.1
-2	-1						13.6
-1	0						34.1
0	1						34.1
1	2						13.6
2	3						2.1
3	4						0

Name _____   Date _____

3. Determine the fit to the normal curve for "High school students perception of the ease with which they could get cocaine powder (V1782)" Use the worksheet on the following page to make your assessment.

Comparison for weak Distribution	% Observed	% Expected
+/- 1 SD		68
+/- 2 SD		95
+/- 3 SD		99.75%

Interpretation of results:

Codebook information		Statistics	
Variable name		Mean	
Variable label		SD	
Minimum		Variance	
Maximum		Range	
Metric		Valid cases	
Level of Measurement			

Class intervals						Distribution	
Continuous z-score		Continuous raw score		Discrete raw score		% of cases per interval	
Lower	Upper	Lower	Upper	Lower	Upper	Observed	Expected
-4	-3						0
-3	-2						2.1
-2	-1						13.6
-1	0						34.1
0	1						34.1
1	2						13.6
2	3						2.1
3	4						0

Name _____   Date _____

4.   Determine the fit to the normal curve for "a variable of your choice"   Use the worksheet
      on the following page to make your assessment.

Comparison for weak Distribution	% Observed	% Expected
+/- 1 SD		68
+/- 2 SD		95
+/- 3 SD		99.75%

Interpretation of results:

Codebook information		Statistics	
Variable name		Mean	
Variable label		SD	
Minimum		Variance	
Maximum		Range	
Metric		Valid cases	
Level of Measurement			

Class intervals						Distribution	
Continuous z-score		Continuous raw score		Discrete raw score		% of cases per interval	
Lower	Upper	Lower	Upper	Lower	Upper	Observed	Expected
-4	-3						0
-3	-2						2.1
-2	-1						13.6
-1	0						34.1
0	1						34.1
1	2						13.6
2	3						2.1
3	4						0

Name _____   **Date** _____

Compare the frequency distribution of a standardized score with the raw scores from question 3. Find and circle the equivalent parts of the frequency distribution for x=2 and z=?.

5. Frequency distribution for ZV1782.

6. Frequency distribution for ZV1782. ZV1782 is a new variable that will be located as the last variable in the dataset.

Name _____   **Date** _____

7. Use Fox's Statistics calculator to convert the raw scores for ease of obtaining cocaine powder (1 to 5) into z-scores. Use the mean and SD which you already have from question 3.

8. Draw a curve showing the approximate shape of the distribution of High School Students perception of the ease of obtaining cocaine powder with the z-scores and raw scores labeled on the graph.

CONFIDENCE INTERVALS

INTRODUCTION

Researchers very often would like to draw conclusions about large populations using information from a sample. You've undoubtably seen the end product of the calculation of a confidence interval whether it was published in a newspaper or in a government publication. For example, a study in 2002 found that "66 percent of Americans favor the death penalty for murderers and this result is accurate within 4 percentage points." Or, you could be reading the results from the *National Crime Victimization Survey* which reports that, in 2004, U.S. residents age 12 or older experienced approximately 24.0 million crimes: 77% (18.6 million) were property crimes, and 21% (5.2 million) were crimes of violence, and 1% were personal thefts (Bureau of Justice Statistics, 2005).

Researchers use statistics derived from samples to make two kinds of estimates about population parameters: point and interval estimates. A point estimate is a single number which is presented as a best guess for the parameter. An interval estimate is a range of values in which we can state with a degree of confidence that we believe we have identified the parameter. There are several kinds of population parameters. This chapter focuses on confidence intervals of means and proportions.

In Levin and Fox, Chapter 6 introduces the concept of the sampling distribution of means. We know, because of sampling variability, that the sample statistic may differ from the population parameter. That is, a researcher expects to make some error in estimating a population parameter when using a sample. As social science researchers we would like to be able to say what the population parameter is while allowing for some error. Researchers will typically give a range of values in which they expect the parameter to fall. The essential question comes down to what is the size of the interval? If the range is too small we will be wrong in stating that we have included the parameter. If it is too large, we may not be saying much about the parameter. The concept of a confidence interval and the procedures for estimating it assist us in identifying an appropriate size.

Confidence intervals

We use the standard error to establish the range of interval estimates. The range of values constructed about the **point estimate** (the mean) is described as the **confidence interval**. The **precision** of the estimate of an interval is the size of the interval. The **level of confidence** in the estimate refers to the probability that the estimate will contain the population parameter. Assuming that sampling errors of the mean are normally distributed, we use the area under the normal curve to estimate the population parameter. The probability of being wrong is called **alpha** (α = 1- confidence level). Social science researchers, by convention, choose either a 90%,

95% or 99% confidence interval. Using a 95% confidence interval means that alpha is 5%. Another way to say this is that a researcher runs the chance of being wrong 5 times in 100 in saying that a confidence interval contains the population parameter.

The formula for confidence intervals for means is below:

$$confidence\ interval = \mu \pm z\frac{\sigma}{\sqrt{N}}$$

The items in the above formula have been used in Chapters 2, 3, and 4. The mean and standard deviation of the mean are information that we get by drawing a sample from a population. Looking at the N in the formula, notice that the precision of an estimate of a parameter would increase if N was larger. Also, the size of the interval will depend on the level of confidence that is chosen because z-scores get larger for greater levels of confidence.

Can we use the above formula to calculate a confidence interval for the American population using sample data from the Monitoring the Future Study, or the General Social Survey? No. These are sample surveys and the above formula requires a *population* standard deviation. However, we can estimate the standard error of the mean using the *sample* standard deviation in place of the *population* standard deviation, and we can use a *t*-distribution instead of a *z*-distribution. The t-distribution takes variations in z-scores by accounting for sample sizes. Go to a t-scores table in Appendix C of Levin and Fox. The t and z-scores look very much the same for large samples (N > 120). As the sample size (N) increases, the t-distribution begins to look like the normal distribution of z-scores. This may sound complicated but it really is not. The revised formula is below:

$$confidence\ interval = \bar{x} \pm t\frac{s}{\sqrt{N-1}}$$

What decisions do we have using data in this workbook? Since we will use the data from the MTF and the GSS, we do not have an opportunity to increase the N (we're using their data; we don't want to do another study). Nonetheless, we will select a level of confidence. The mathematics looks complicated but confidence intervals are quite simple to explain to a non-statistical person once the results are calculated.

DATA ANALYSIS EXAMPLE 1

Research problem: Calculate an interval estimate of the number of hours per data that Americans watch television. We will use the General Social Survey to make a 95% confidence interval estimate of the population parameter for respondent's income for **all** American adults in the United States in 2004.

Codebook information: Use the codebook to get basic information on the level of measurement for the variable (RINCOM98). The codebook simply tells us that the variable is recorded as a scale ranging from less than $1,000 (1) to over $100,000 (23) with "Don't Know (98)," "Refused (24 and 99)," and "Question not Asked (0)" excluded as missing values. In order to calculate a confidence interval we will treat this as an scalar variable with a metric of 1 unit of income.

Calculating a confidence interval: SPSS for windows calculates confidence intervals for single variables where you may select any level of confidence. By convention, we will most often use the 95 percent confidence interval, sometimes 99, and less often the 90 percent interval.

There are several ways to get SPSS to calculate a confidence interval. Let's use the ONE SAMPLE T TEST in which we will set the options 90, 95, and then 99 percent. To get this information, click on ANALYZE, move down to COMPARE MEANS, and then select the ONE SAMPLE T-TEST.

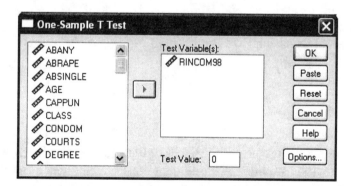

Our test variable from above is "RINCOM98." By default, a 95% confidence interval will be generated. Click on "Options" to change it to 90 and then 99 to complete the exercises.

Depending upon the statistical program (and the version of SPSS), some programs give descriptive information such as the mean and standard deviation. We will need to look for the appropriate parts that we wish to use in our interpretation.

One-Sample Statistics

	N	Mean	Std. Deviation	Std. Error Mean
RINCOM98 RESPONDENTS INCOME	919	14.26	5.653	.186

One-Sample Test

	Test Value = 0					
					95% Confidence Interval of the Difference	
	t	df	Sig. (2-tailed)	Mean Difference	Lower	Upper
RINCOM98 RESPONDENTS INCOME	76.489	918	.000	14.263	13.90	14.63

We see that 919 persons answered the question. The mean score is reported as 14.26 with a standard deviation of 5.653. We are not overly interested in this part of the output as we are looking for the "interval" estimate.

The one-sample t-test shows the confidence interval. Note that it states the level of confidence is 95%. You can adjust this to any level. The right side of the output shows the lower and upper limits as 13.90 and 14.63. The width of the interval (potential size of error) is not provided but it can easily be determined using a hand calculation to see the size of the confidence interval (14.63 - 13.90 = .73 units of income). It is always a good idea to look back into a codebook to determine what these values mean so that we can provide a summary of these results.

Interpretation: The General Social Survey (2004) asked adult Americans about their personal income. This income is converted into 1998 dollars so that results from the 2004 survey can be compared with previous studies. A 95 percent confidence interval was calculated. We are 95% confident that the average individual income of Americans falls no lower than 13.90 units and no higher that 14.63 units. These lower and upper boundaries round to values of 14 and 15. A value of 14 corresponds with $22,500-$24,999 and a 15 is $24,999-$29,999. Hence, we are 95 percent confident that an Average American's individual income falls between $22,500 and $29,999 standardized in 1998 dollars. This confidence interval is based upon 918 completed interviews of adult Americans in 2004.

DATA ANALYSIS EXAMPLE 2

Many studies include questions with "yes" or "no" type questions. This is a nominal level variable with two categories. A confidence interval can be used to estimate the percentage of responses. Levin and Fox, in Chapter 6, discuss the formula for confidence intervals using proportions.

Research problem: Calculate an interval estimate of percentage of students in American High Schools that have ever had alcoholic beverages (v103). We will use the Monitoring the Future Study to make a 95% confidence interval estimate of the population parameter for **all** American students in grade 12 in the United States in 2004.

Codebook information: Note that no=1 and yes = 2. This is a nominal level variable with two categories. It is appropriate to calculate a confidence interval.

Computer output: The results of the analysis are shown below.

One-Sample Statistics

	N	Mean	Std. Deviation	Std. Error Mean
v103 042B03!:EVER DRINK	1435	1.76	.427	.011

One-Sample Test

	Test Value = 0					
					95% Confidence Interval of the Difference	
	t	df	Sig. (2-tailed)	Mean Difference	Lower	Upper
v103 042B03!:EVER DRINK	156.141	1434	.000	1.760	1.74	1.78

From the codebook, a "1" means that a student does not drink and a "2" means that they do drink. A simple trick to make the 1 and 2 more intuitive is to turn them into 0 (no) and 1 (yes). We will subtract 1 from the interval estimate. Alternatively, you could recode the variables to zeros and ones before calculating the interval.

The lower estimate is shown as 1.74 and the upper estimate is 1.78. Subtract 1.00 from each and it is now 0.74 and 0.78. Convert them to percentages by multiplying the proportions by 100. This yields a result of 74% to 78%. These are the lower and upper bounds on the

115

percentage of American high school students that have ever had a drink of beer, wine, wine coolers and liquor. What is the interval size?   The answer is 78-74 or 4 percent.

Interpretation: Based on the Monitoring the Future Study (2004) which studies high school seniors in the United States, we are 95% confident that between 74 and 78 percent of American high school seniors in 2004 have ever had a drink of alcohol. The question on the survey asked "Have you ever had any beer, wine, wine coolers, or liquor to drink?" The response categories were yes or no.

Another common way to present results is to report the point estimate and the amount of error (one half of the interval size goes on either side of the point estimate). In this case we would say that we estimate that about 76 percent of students have ever had a drink (look at the Mean of 1.76 in the first table). These results are accurate plus or minus 2 percent 19 times in 20 (Question: What is 19 /20?; Answer: it is another way to say 95% confidence).

When writing up the results of a confidence interval, a good summary will:
- State the source of information;
- Describe the measurement of the variable;
- Indicate the level of confidence; and
- Report either the lower and upper limits of the interval; or the point estimate and the amount of error.

KEY TERMS

Confidence interval
Error
Interval estimate
Point estimate
Precision

Web-sites:

The Bureau of Justice Statistics: www.ojp.usdoj.gov/bjs/
    Follow the links to the National Crime Victimization Survey. You can get a description of the survey and access the full reports.

The Gallup Organization: www.gallup.com
    The Gallup organization conducts public opinion polls on a variety of social issues.

Name _____   Date _____

1.   Using the Monitoring the Future Study, calculate 90%, 95%, and 99% confidence
        interval estimates on American High School students' perception of the risk of five or
        more drinks once or twice each weekend (V1779).

Codebook information:

Use the ONE-SAMPLE T-TEST procedure in SPSS to calculate confidence intervals. Record
the information in the table below. Use hand-calculations to obtain the interval width for each
group.

Confidence	Frequency	Mean	SD	Lower limit	Upper limit	Interval size
90						
95						
99						

Interpret one of the confidence intervals for the sample.

Explain what happens to the size of the interval as the level of confidence increases.

Name _____   **Date** _____

2.   Using the General Social Survey, calculate 90%, 95%, and 99% confidence interval estimates on Americans with guns in their household (OWNGUN).

Codebook information:

Use the ONE-SAMPLE T-TEST procedure in SPSS to calculate confidence intervals. Record the information in the table below. Use hand-calculations to obtain the interval width for each group.

Confidence	Frequency	Mean	SD	Lower limit	Upper limit	Interval size
90						
95						
99						

Interpret one of the confidence intervals for the sample.

Explain what happens to the size of the interval as the level of confidence increases.

Name _____   **Date** _____

3.   Choose a variable from either the Monitoring the Future Survey or the General Social Survey. Remember it has to be an interval level variable or a dichotomous variable. Calculate 90%, 95%, and 99% confidence interval estimates.

Codebook information:

Use the ONE-SAMPLE T-TEST procedure in SPSS to calculate confidence intervals. Record the information in the table below. Use hand-calculations to obtain the interval width for each group.

Confidence	Frequency	Mean	SD	Lower limit	Upper limit	Interval size
90						
95						
99						

Interpret one of the confidence intervals for the sample.

Explain what happens to the size of the interval as the level of confidence increases.

Name _____   Date _____

4. Use your college library to find two research articles about public opinion on binge drinking. Use these articles to compare and discuss results from high school seniors.

5. For the following data, use Fox's Statistics Calculator (Confidence intervals from raw data) to calculate a mean, standard deviation, and a 95 percent confidence interval.

    Casinos are an interesting phenomenon. We asked fifteen people exiting the casino about how much they had won or lost tonight in the casino. The results (in dollars) are reported below

    -85, -55, - 65, -180, +5, +120, -45, -25, -20, -80, +45, -30, -50, +50, -25

    Mean = _____

    SD = _____

    95% Confidence interval = _____ to _____

    Interpretation

T-TESTS

INTRODUCTION

A t-test is used to examine the relationship between a dependent variable measured at the interval (or ratio) level and a nominal level independent variable with two categories (dichotomous). In this chapter you will:

1.   go through the steps of hypothesis testing;
2.   use t-tests to examine the form, extent, and statistical significance of a t-test.

T-TESTS

Suppose you are interested in public perceptions of sexual mores. The General Social Survey includes a variety of questions on attitudes toward pre-marital sex, extra-marital sex, pornography, and other issues. A researcher suggests that men and women will differ in their attitudes about pre-marital sex. We would like to do a statistical test to determine whether or not this statement is accurate.

Levels of Measurement

The dependent variable for our analysis is whether or not a person views sex before marriage as wrong (PREMARSX). This is a scalar (interval) variable ranging from always wrong (1) to not wrong at all (4). For this test, let's assume that the metric is continuous ranging with a metric of one-unit of wrongness.

The independent variable for our study is sex of the respondent (Sex). This is a nominal level variable with two categories: Male (1) and Female (2).

Form

The form of the relationship in a t-test refers to the directional difference between means. If there is a significant difference in the means we will look at the descriptive statistics to identify which group is higher or lower.

Extent

The extent of the relationship in a t-test simply refers to how much of a difference there is comparing the mean for females to the mean for males.

Level of significance

We will use the t-test to test whether or not there is a difference between the mean of wrongness of pre-marital sex comparing females to males. Before proceeding we must choose a level of significance. This is a benchmark of how large the difference in means must be for us to accept that there is a statistical difference. Traditionally, social researchers use either a 95% or 99% level of confidence in results. This means that the alpha level of error will be 5% or 1%. This is usually expressed as a proportion of .05 or .01. In this example we will work using a 95% confidence level or $\alpha = .05$.

DATA ANALYSIS EXAMPLE

Research Problem:

Hypothesis testing: Write out the research, null and alternative hypotheses for a t-test.

Note that the null hypothesis (null means zero or none) is a statement that there is no difference between sample means. The research hypothesis, on the other hand, suggests that there will be a difference.

In our example, we're going to find out whether women and men have different opinions about whether pre-marital sex is wrong. How are the variables coded? We need to look at the codebook to make our prediction on the direction. Sex of the respondent (Sex) is coded as male (1) and female (2). The degree of wrongness of premarital sex (Premarsx) is coded as Not wrong at all (4) to always wrong (1). The null and research hypotheses are shown below.

T-Test of difference between means

	$\alpha = .05$
Null Hypothesis: Men and women will have the same opinion about premarital sex.	$\mu_1 = \mu_2$
Research Hypothesis: Men and women will differ in their opinions About premarital sex.	$\mu_1 \neq \mu_2$

The t-test procedure in SPSS is calculated by clicking on ANALYZE, COMPARE MEANS, and the INDEPENDENT-SAMPLES T Test.   Our "dependent" or "test" variable is **PREMARSX**. Click on W1 in the variable list and then move it to the test variable box. The "grouping" or "independent" variable is **SEX**. Move it across and then click on "Define groups." From the codebook, we know that men are 1 and women are 2. Click on OK to execute the t-test.

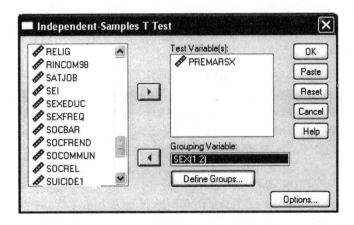

The computer output for the t-test is shown below. The first table shows descriptive statistics for Males (group 1) and Females (Group 2). It is a good idea to look at this table because it will show if you have entered the dependent and independent variables in the correct boxes. If it showed 1 Always wrong and 2 Almost always wrong in the group statistics then you should immediately note that you need to redo the analysis (A common error for first time users).

Group Statistics

	SEX RESPONDENTS SEX	N	Mean	Std. Deviation	Std. Error Mean
PREMARSX SEX BEFORE MARRIAGE	1 MALE	216	3.03	1.214	.083
	2 FEMALE	239	2.67	1.289	.083

Independent Samples Test

	Levene's Test for Equality of Variances		t-test for Equality of Means							
									95% Confidence Interval of the Difference	
	F	Sig.	t	df	Sig. (2-tailed)	Mean Difference	Std. Error Difference	Lower	Upper
PREMARSX SE) Equal variance BEFORE MARRI/ assumed	7.194	.008	3.119	453	.002	.367	.118	.136	.598
Equal variance not assumed			3.129	452.217	.002	.367	.117	.137	.598

Next, look to the lower table where you'll see two types of t-tests: Equal variances assumed and equal variances not assumed. Thinking back to Chapter 3, what is variance? It's related to standard deviations. In essence, the computer is looking to see whether the variation in male scores is the same (equal) to the variation for female scores. Look at the standard deviations in this example (1.21 male; 1.289 female). Are they about the same? They look close, but the Levene's F-test tells us that the variation (s^2) for men and women is really different. Using an alpha level of .05, we look to the F-ratio and make a decision about which t-test to read. In this case, F=7.2, p<.05. If the probability is less than .05 we use the unequal test. If the probability is greater than .05 (p>.05) then we would have used an equal test. Here the Levene's test is significant so that we will use the unequal variances t-test (Equal variances not assumed). The computer prints both so that the researcher can do the analysis in one step.

The t-value for the equal variances not assumed is 3.129. A two-tailed probability is printed by default. To determine significance we look to see whether the significance is less than our pre-determined alpha level. It is less than α =.05. Hence, we reject the null hypothesis. The results of your research should be written into a summary notation as follows:

$$t \ (df) = \text{value}, \text{p-level (either p<.05 or p>.05)}$$

The degrees of freedom for the test are printed in the output. Round the degrees of freedom to the nearest whole number.

In this example the result of the t-test is: t (452) = 3.1, p < .05.

We have found a significant difference in the means for men and women. We reject the null hypothesis that men and women have identical views on pre-marital sex in favor of the research hypothesis that woman will differ from men in whether they will say pre-marital sex is wrong. We now need to go back to the means for women and men to interpret the form and extent of the difference.

124

The descriptive statistics table reports the means as: Male = 3.03 and Female= 2.67. The mean for males is a larger number which suggests than men are less likely than women to say that premarital sex is wrong. How much less? Simply subtract 2.67 – 3.03 to get -.36 units. The extent of the difference is .36 units of the metric which we will call .36 units of wrongness. We're ready to write up our summary of the entire analysis.

Interpretation:

An analysis of the 2004 General Social Survey shows that women are significantly more likely than men to say that pre-marital sex is wrong. Response categories on this question were not at all (4), sometimes (3), almost always (2) and always (1) wrong. We used an F-test (F= 7.2, p<.05) to select an unequal variance t-test. The difference in means in significant (t (452)= 3.1, p<.05). The form of the relationship is that women (M=2.67) are more likely than men (M=3.03) to say that pre-marital sex is wrong. The extent of the difference is .36 units of wrongfulness. This difference in means is large enough that we reject the null hypothesis of no differences in means about worry at a .05 level of significance. However, while we have found a *significant* difference between men and women, this is not a *substantively* large difference in the means. We find that the average for American women and men is such that both sexes would say that pre-marital sex is sometimes wrong.

When writing up the results of a t-test, a good summary will:

- State the source of information;
- Describe the measurement of the dependent variable and state which groups are being compared;
- Indicate the level of confidence;
- State the decision on the null hypothesis as reject or fail to reject; and
- Discuss the form and extent of the difference (when the null hypothesis is rejected).

KEY TERMS

Alternative hypothesis
equal variances assumed
equal variances not assumed
Levine's F-test
Null hypothesis
Research hypothesis
Significance
t-test

Name _____   **Date** _____

1. *Research Problems:* Use the Monitoring the Future study to compare marijuana use in the past 30 days by sex.

Research hypothesis: There will be a difference in marijuana use by sex of the student. (V117 and V150)

Write out the null and research hypothesis

Which t-test? Explain your choice

The results:

Write out a brief interpretation

Name _____   **Date** _____

2.   *Research Problems:* Use the Monitoring the Future study to test a hypothesis:

Choose a nominal level 2-N independent variable and an appropriate dependent variable.

Write out the null and research hypothesis

Which t-test? Explain your choice

The results:

Write out a brief interpretation

Name _____ **Date** _____

3. *Research Problems:* Use the General Social Survey, 2004.

Research hypothesis: Respondent's income will vary by their sex. (Rincom98 and sex)

Write out the null and research hypothesis

Which t-test? Explain your choice

The results:

Write out a brief interpretation

Name _____   **Date** _____

4.   *Research Problems:* Use the General Social Survey, 2004.

Research hypothesis: Respondent's socioeconomic index will vary by their sex. (SEI and sex)

Write out the null and research hypothesis

Which t-test? Explain your choice

The results:

Write out a brief interpretation

129

Name _____　　　**Date** _____

5.　　*Research Problems:* Use the General Social Survey, 2004.

Choose a nominal level 2-N independent variable and an appropriate dependent variable.

Write out the null and research hypothesis

Which t-test? Explain your choice

The results:

Write out a brief interpretation

Name _____   **Date** _____

Use Fox's Statistics Calculator to calculate t-tests for the following problems.

6. A researcher is interested in the effect of violent video games on attitudes toward domestic violence. Sixteen subjects (independent samples) who volunteered for an extra-credit lab exercise at their university were told that they were selected to be part of a project on video games and family life. Eight of them played a video game that included explicit images of violence images. The other eight played a non-violent video game. All subjects were then taken to a room where they were asked to play the video game for 30 minutes before completing the experiment. Both groups completed a survey which included a question on attitudes toward family violence (1=not at all to 10 = hitting a woman is sometimes okay). The family violence scale for people in each group was recorded and is presented below. The null hypothesis is that there will be no difference in the attitudes toward family violence between people in the two different video game conditions.

> Violent video: 2, 2, 4, 7, 5, 2, 4, 5
> Non-violent video: 1, 3, 2, 2, 4, 3, 1, 1

a.   Write out a research hypothesis.

b.   What is the mean level of tolerance for family violence in the violent video sample?
       _____

       … for the non-violent video sample? _____

c.   What are the standard deviations for each group? SD (High) = _____

       …. SD (Low) = _____

d.   Calculate the standard error of the difference between the means. _____

e.   Calculate the t-ratio. _____

f.   Determine the degrees of freedom. _____

g.   Assume an alpha of .05. What is the critical score or ratio? _____

h.   Do you reject or fail to reject the null hypothesis? _____

i.   Write an interpretation of the results.

Name _____   **Date** _____

7. Dr. Williams develops an hypothesis. She feels that after fours years of college that a person's self-perception should be different. Dr. Williams randomly selects 6 students just starting college and administers an Opinion of Self Perception Test (OSPT). Four years later, she administers the OSPT to these same students. The results are:

Year 1	Year 4
13	18
12	17
14	11
11	20
8	21
12	19

a.   Are these samples related? Explain.

b.   What is the null hypothesis?

c.   What is the research hypothesis?

d.   What is the standard deviation of the distribution of difference scores? _____

e.   What is the standard error of the mean difference? _____

f.   Assume an alpha of .05. What is the critical t-value? _____

g.   What is the value of the t-test? _____

h.   What is Dr. Williams' research decision?

ANALYSIS OF VARIANCE (ANOVA)

INTRODUCTION

Males versus females, parents versus children, and delinquent versus non-delinquent are some of the many two-sample comparisons that we may wish to make in understanding social behavior. However, group variation goes beyond simple dichotomies.

Researchers will often need to make comparisons of three or more samples or groups. For example, you may wish to compare people of different marital status (Married, Widowed, Single, Divorced or Separated), or of different geographical regions (Northeast, Northcentral, South, and West) to determine whether an independent variable is statistically related to a dependent variable such as attitudes toward marijuana use.

This chapter introduces you to analysis of variance (ANOVA) to test the situation where you have an interval (or ratio) level dependent variable and a nominal level independent variable with three or more groups. The independent variable, in fact, may actually be measured at a higher level of measurement (ordinal, interval, or ratio) but ANOVA simply treats it as a nominal variable.

You may be wondering why we don't just do a series of t-tests to compare the means in the groups. The t-test assumes that independent samples are drawn from a population. If we make more than one comparison, the groups would not be from independent samples. Thus, we need a more sophisticated test.

ANALYSIS OF VARIANCE

This chapter will use the one-way analysis of variance procedure (ONE-WAY ANOVA). The ONE-WAY procedure is the simplest type of ANOVA for understanding bivariate relationships.

Form

Unlike a t-test, where there is just one comparison, an ANOVA may have multiple groups for comparison. The form of the relationship in ONEWAY is a description of the pattern of differences in the means.

Extent

The extent of the relationship in an ANOVA is identical to that of a t-test where you describe the magnitude of differences in the means.

Level of significance

We will use $\alpha = .05$ as the criterion for significance in the example.

DATA ANALYSIS EXAMPLE

Research Problem: Is there a statistical relationship between the a person's socioeconomic status and their marital status?

We will use a one-way analysis of variance test to examine this question using a sample of Americans from the 2004 General Social Survey.

Codebook information: Use the codebook to get basic information about each variable. We will assume that respondent's socioeconomic index (SEI) is a scalar level variable. The following table identifies the characteristics of each variable:

Variable(s) and value(s)				
Dependent variable			**Independent variable**	
Variable name	SEI		Variable name	MARITAL
Variable Label	R's socioeconomic index		Variable label	R's marital status
Minimum category (value)	17 = lowest possible status		Minimum Category (value)	1= Married
Maximum category (value)	97.2 highest possible status		Maximum Category (value)	5= Never married
Level of measurement	Scalar		Level of measurement	nominal
Metric	1 unit of prestige		Metric	n.a.

Hypothesis: Write out the null hypothesis and research hypothesis for the research problem.

ONEWAY Analysis of Variance

	$\alpha = .05$
Null Hypothesis: None of the group means will differ	$\mu_1 = \mu_2 = \mu_3 = \mu_4 = \mu_5$

Alternative Hypothesis:
      A person's socioeconomic index will
      be related to their marital status.
	some $\mu_i \neq \mu_j$
	
	(two-tailed test)

The oneway analysis of variance procedure provides an omnibus test, the F-ratio, of whether or not at least one of the means ($\mu_i ... \mu_j$) differs from the other means. The F-ratio and its derivation is discussed in greater detail in Chapter 8 of Levin and Fox.

To Generate the basic output, select ANALYZE, COMPARE MEANS, and then One-Way ANOVA. The basic dialogue box is shown below. The dependent variable is entered into the dependent list and the independent variable is entered as a "factor." We also need to select out "options" and "post hoc" test(s). In options, check "descriptive" in the statistics box. In Post Hoc, select the "Tukey" test. A large variety of range tests are available but Tukey's Honestly Significant Differences (HSD) is a commonly used test. An advanced course in ANOVA is required to explain the nuances for each range test.

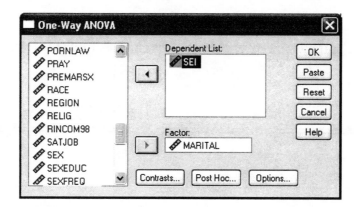

Computer output (one way analysis of variance):

ANOVA

SEI RESPONDENT SOCIOECONOMIC INDEX

	Sum of Squares	df	Mean Square	F	Sig.
Between Groups	11444.367	4	2861.092	7.508	.000
Within Groups	535013.7	1404	381.064		
Total	546458.1	1408			

The F-ratio is printed in the output of the Summary ANOVA table as 7.508. A variety of notations to summarize the F-ratio are used in the literature. Most social science publications use the format of the American Psychological Association (APA). It is important to use a consistent notation reporting statistics, the degrees of freedom, a rounded-off value, and the probability level:

General form: F (df-between, df-within) = value, p-level (p<.05, or p>.05).

In our example: F (4, 1404) = 7.5, p<.05

Interpretation of F-Ratio:

Our analysis shows that there is a statistically significant relationship between a person's socioeconomic index and their marital status. ($F_{(4, 1404)} = 7.5$, $p < .05$)

Since there is a significant relationship, we may proceed to conduct multiple range tests. The F-ratio does not tell us which means differ from each other, nor does it tell us by how much they differ. We need to conduct additional "post hoc" analysis of these data to determine where the differences exist.

Multiple comparison tests

Since the F-ratio is significant (we reject the null hypothesis that each of the group means are equal) we proceed to conduct multiple comparisons of the means. If the F-ratio was not significant we would not conduct these tests. There are a wide variety of range tests. We checked Tukey as an option for post hoc comparisons of means.

Multiple Comparisons

Dependent Variable: SEI RESPONDENT SOCIOECONOMIC INDEX

Tukey HSD

(I) MARITAL MARITAL STATUS	(J) MARITAL MARITAL STATUS	Mean Difference (I-J)	Std. Error	Sig.	95% Confidence Interval	
					Lower Bound	Upper Bound
1 MARRIED	2 WIDOWED	5.2357	2.0963	.092	-.490	10.961
	3 DIVORCED	4.1980	1.5378	.050	-.002	8.398
	4 SEPARATED	8.3828*	2.9349	.035	.367	16.399
	5 NEVER MARRIED	6.0205*	1.3234	.000	2.406	9.635
2 WIDOWED	1 MARRIED	-5.2357	2.0963	.092	-10.961	.490
	3 DIVORCED	-1.0377	2.3973	.993	-7.586	5.510
	4 SEPARATED	3.1470	3.4635	.894	-6.313	12.607
	5 NEVER MARRIED	.7847	2.2658	.997	-5.404	6.973
3 DIVORCED	1 MARRIED	-4.1980	1.5378	.050	-8.398	.002
	2 WIDOWED	1.0377	2.3973	.993	-5.510	7.586
	4 SEPARATED	4.1847	3.1570	.675	-4.438	12.807
	5 NEVER MARRIED	1.8224	1.7619	.839	-2.990	6.635
4 SEPARATED	1 MARRIED	-8.3828*	2.9349	.035	-16.399	-.367
	2 WIDOWED	-3.1470	3.4635	.894	-12.607	6.313
	3 DIVORCED	-4.1847	3.1570	.675	-12.807	4.438
	5 NEVER MARRIED	-2.3623	3.0583	.939	-10.715	5.991
5 NEVER MARRIED	1 MARRIED	-6.0205*	1.3234	.000	-9.635	-2.406
	2 WIDOWED	-.7847	2.2658	.997	-6.973	5.404
	3 DIVORCED	-1.8224	1.7619	.839	-6.635	2.990
	4 SEPARATED	2.3623	3.0583	.939	-5.991	10.715

*. The mean difference is significant at the .05 level.

A multiple comparison test is interpreted like a t-test where two groups are compared to each other. Unfortunately SPSS does not provide a conventional summary table of results. The usual procedure is to arrange the means from lowest to highest and then to calculate whether or not they are significantly different from each other. Fortunately, though, the computer program does make all of these comparisons.

A conventional table can be rebuilt based on the following steps:

1) Using the "Descriptives," arrange the means from the lowest to the highest value. The "Descriptives" were obtained by checking its box in "Options."
2) Record the N's for each group.
3) Place an asterisk beside comparisons where the mean difference in values is significant at $\alpha = .05$.
4) Draw –'s on the diagonal where variables are compared to themselves (e.g. 2 to 2); and
5) By APA convention, only the upper half of the multiple comparison table is completed.

Descriptives

SEI RESPONDENT SOCIOECONOMIC INDEX

	N	Mean	Std. Deviation	Std. Error	95% Confidence Interval for Mean		Minimum	Maximum
					Lower Bound	Upper Bound		
1 MARRIED	753	53.355	19.8643	.7239	51.934	54.776	17.1	97.2
2 WIDOWED	98	48.119	20.4283	2.0636	44.024	52.215	17.1	89.2
3 DIVORCED	205	49.157	18.4576	1.2891	46.615	51.699	21.2	97.2
4 SEPARATED	47	44.972	19.6101	2.8604	39.215	50.730	21.2	87.9
5 NEVER MARRIED	306	47.335	19.0439	1.0887	45.192	49.477	17.1	97.2
Total	1409	50.793	19.7005	.5248	49.764	51.823	17.1	97.2

Let's take a moment to look at the means in the descriptives table. What is the average socioeconomic index (SEI) for married persons? The computer output shows a mean of 53.355 which we will round to 53.4. Have a look at the descriptives above and find the mean for each of the other group's mean scores.

We will need to arrange these mean scores from lowest to highest so that we can construct the multiple range test table. The lowest mean score is 45.0 for separated, 47.3 for never married, and so on. Record the group and label, the group N, and the mean value in the multiple range test table.

Multiple comparison test: Tukey's HSD							
Group/Label	N	Mean (smallest to largest)	4	5	2	3	1
4 Separated	47	45.0	--				*
5 Never married	306	47.3		--			*
2 Widowed	98	48.1			--		
3 Divorced	205	49.2				--	
1 Married	753	53.4					--
			Significant differences * = p< .05				

Next, we want to find out which groups are significantly different from each other. Working in the rows in the new table, we will start with separated. Look back in the SPSS computer output to the table labeled as multiple comparisons. Find separated in the table and look to see if there are any asterisks in this blocking. Do you see any? Yes, there is one asterisk beside married in this comparison. Mark an asterisk in the new table in row 1 moving across to married (group 1) at the end of the row. Next, move to never married in row 2. Look at never married in the computer output. Are there any asterisks? Yes; in one case beside married. Place an asterisk across from never married and under # 1 for married. Look next at widowed in the multiple comparison output. Are there any significant differences? No. Move to divorced and notice that there are no differences. Lastly, for married we see that there are two significant differences comparing married to separated and to never married. We skip these asterisks because they would go on the lower side of the matrix. We would do the same on any other asterisks that may have gone on the lower side of the matrix. By convention only the upper half of the table is completed. We still know that separated and never married persons differ from married persons because of the asterisks in column 5 of the table. Remember that only the upper half of the table is completed.

To finish the table, write a key at the bottom showing that significant differences at the

.05 level are marked with an asterisk. A .05 level is the default level in SPSS and it shown at the bottom of the table of multiple comparisons.

Interpretation of Multiple Comparison tests:

Each asterisk in the output refers to a significant difference at the .05 level between two means. For example, the first asterisk in row one shows that the average SEI of 45.0 for separated persons is significantly different than the average SEI of 53.4 for married persons. The extent of the differences in means (53.4 – 45.0 is 8.4 units of socioeconomic status). The difference in these means tells us how much of an difference in SEI there is between groups.

Each blank space in the table tells us that there are no significant differences between groups. For example, divorced persons averaged 49.2 and never married persons averaged 47.3 but the extent of the difference is not large enough to be significantly different. In other examples, you may see instances that might look like a large difference, but remember that it could also be that there are too few persons in a group for us to be confident that there is a reliable difference. The post hoc test takes the sample sizes into account as it calculates the significance of differences. A computer program will use its bank of calculations of Tukey's test and tell us whether a difference in means is significant at the .05 level.

There are a large number of comparisons that are possible in this multiple comparison table. You should familiarize yourself with reading and drawing multiple range tables (when a table is appropriate). A full interpretation involves drawing out some of the comparisons to suggest why the analysis is important.

Summary interpretation:

The 2004 General Social Survey was used to test whether socioeconomic status of Americans differs by marital status. People's socioeconomic status was evaluated using a standardized scale ranging from 17 to 97 with higher numbers indicating higher status. Marital status was measured as Married (1), Widowed (2), Divorced (3), Separated (4), and Never-married (5). Using a One-way ANOVA, we reject the null hypothesis that the means were equal based on $F(4, 1404) = 7.5$, $p<.05$. A Tukey's HSD test, shown in the table above, shows which pairs are significantly different. Notably, people who are married have significantly higher average socioeconomic index scores than people who are never married and people who are separated. Married persons averaged 53.4 points on the index and scored about 6 points higher than never married persons and 8 points higher than separated persons. No other pairings were significantly different at the .05 level of significance.

When writing up the results of an ANOVA test, a good summary will:

- State the source of information;
- Describe the measurement of the dependent variable and state which groups are being compared;
- Indicate the level of confidence;
- State the decision on the null hypothesis as reject or fail to reject.
- A multiple comparison table should be included if there are a large number of groups; and
- Discuss the form and extent of differences when the null hypothesis is rejected.

KEY TERMS

American Psychological Association: APA format
ANOVA
ANOVA summary table
Descriptives
F-Ratio
Mean Square
Multiple comparison test
One-way
Post hoc test
Sum of squares
Tukey's HSD (Honestly Significant Difference)

Name _____   **Date** _____

Research Problems: Use a One-way analysis of variance to test the following hypotheses:

Research hypothesis 1.   Use the General Social Survey to test if political views (POLVIEWS) is statistically related to marital status (Marital).

Summary ANOVA Table

	SS	df	MS	F	Sig
Between					
Within					
Total					

Is the F-Ratio significant?

Post-hoc Table: Tukey's HSD

Interpretation of results

Name _____   **Date** _____

Research Problems: Use a One-way analysis of variance to test the following hypotheses:

Research hypothesis 2.   Select two variables from the General Social Survey to test an
                               hypothesis.

Summary ANOVA Table

	SS	df	MS	F	Sig
Between					
Within					
Total					

Is the F-Ratio significant?

Post-hoc Table: Tukey's HSD

Interpretation of results

Name _____   **Date** _____

Research Problems: Use a One-way analysis of variance to test the following hypotheses:

Research hypothesis 3.   Use the Monitoring the Future Study to test whether satisfaction with personal safety (V1643) varies by School Region (V13).

Summary ANOVA Table

	SS	df	MS	F	Sig
Between					
Within					
Total					

Is the F-Ratio significant?

Post-hoc Table: Tukey's HSD

Interpretation of results

Name _____   **Date** _____

Research Problems: Use a One-way analysis of variance to test the following hypotheses:

Research hypothesis 4.   Select two variables from the Monitoring the Future Study to test an hypothesis.

Write our your hypothesis:

Summary ANOVA Table

	SS	df	MS	F	Sig
Between					
Within					
Total					

Is the F-Ratio significant?

Post-hoc Table: Tukey's HSD

Interpretation of results

Name _____   Date _____

Research Problems: Use Fox's Statistics Calculator to calculate an ANOVA using raw data:

5.   Based on his own experiences in court, a prosecutor believes that some judges provide more severe penalties than others for people convicted for drunk driving. A sample of five of the most recent drunk driving sentences (in months) handed down by each of the three judges are shown below.

Judge #1	Judge # 2	Judge # 3
2	3	13
3	2	15
7	4	20
2	3	10
2	4	10

a.   Test the hypothesis that some judges give longer sentences than others for the same offense at (α =.05).

b.   If appropriate, construct a multiple comparison table. Why/Why not?

c.   Write out an overall summary. If you were advising someone who was about to be sentenced which judge(s) would you want?

CHI-SQUARE

INTRODUCTION

In Chapters 7 and 8, you were introduced to t-tests and analysis of variance. Each of these statistical methods is powerful for testing hypotheses. While both methods are commonly used by social science researchers, it is often difficult to meet the basic assumptions of parametric statistics: (1) normality in a population, and (2) that variables are measured at the interval or ratio level.

Researchers often will be faced with studying the relationships between variables that are nonparametric: (1) samples are not normally distributed, (2) samples are not drawn from a population, and (3) variables are measured at the nominal or ordinal level. In fact, a great deal of social science research fails to meet the assumptions of parametric statistics so that researchers must depend on a variety of nonparametric statistics to test the significance of relationships between variables.

This chapter introduces cross-tabulations for analyzing independence of two variables. Specifically, we use cross-tabulations (cross-tabs) to compare the distribution of one dependent variable across the categories of an independent variable. Both variables must be *discrete* and they usually are measured at the nominal or ordinal level. Chapter 12 shows some options when both variables are ordinal.

A cross-tab usually consists of **two or more** columns and **two or more** rows. (A frequency distribution has **one** column and two or more rows.) The conventional way of building a cross-tab is for the rows to correspond with the dependent variable and the columns correspond with the independent variable. While cross-tabulations may involve two or more variables, this chapter only discusses two-way (or bi-variate) cross-tabs. The use and interpretation of multi-way cross-tabs extends beyond an introduction to statistics.

This chapter will illustrate a **two-way chi-square** test of independence. The chi-square test is perhaps the simplest application for testing the significance of bi-variate relationships when variables are measured at the nominal or ordinal level. We will demonstrate how to measure the form and extent of bi-variate cross-tabular relationships.

CROSS-TABS AND THE CHI-SQUARE TEST

An important aspect of a cross-tab is its size. The convention for describing size is to state the number of rows (r) and columns (c) it contains. For example, we may examine households in the United States with guns (2 categories; yes or no) and sex (2 categories; male or female). The cross-tab will be a two by two (r x c; or 2 x 2) table. Multiplication of the number of rows by columns tells us that there will be four **cells** in the table. The size of the table is very important because many statistics, including chi-square, do not work well when the number of cells is large and the expected number of cases in some cells may be small. Levin and Fox, in Chapter 9, discuss the Yates correction of chi square for the problem of small expected frequencies. SPSS will print the Yate's correction and a warning about the percentage of cells with low expected frequencies when appropriate. Fox's Statistics Calculator shows it as well.

The conventional method for building a cross-tabulation table is to put categories of the dependent variable in the rows and the categories of the independent variable as columns. This is the general method recommended in the *Publication Manual of the American Psychological Association* which. Column percentages are calculated for each cell where the count in each cell is divided by the column total and multiplied by 100. A researcher will "percentage down" and "compare across" columns. If the dependent variable is placed on the top of the table, a row percentage should be used and comparisons will be made by comparing down the column. These kinds of tables are often used when a researcher has developed a table to "fit the page." Try to avoid making these kinds of tables in your own research since they are non-conventional and they may confuse a general reader.

Form and extent

Establishing the form of a cross-tab depends on the size of the table and the level of measurement of the variables. There are many different possible types of cross-tabs. Chi-square is considered as an appropriate statistic when both the dependent and independent variables are at the nominal level, or one of the variables is nominal and the other is ordinal. The discussion below very much simplifies the possibilities for form and extent.

2 x 2 table (row by column)

In a 2 x 2 table both variables can be considered as measured at the nominal level. Column percentages are required to make an assessment of form. The convention for stating form is to subtract the column percentage in the top left cell from the column percentage in the top right cell. The **form** refers to whether the column percentage of the top left cell is **larger or smaller** than the top left cell. The **extent** of the relationship is the **percentage difference** of the two cells.

2 x c table when the independent variable is nominal

The form in a 2 x c table when n is nominal is calculated by comparing each of the column percentages to a reference category. The reference category is determined by the researcher to meet his or her needs. For example, I live in the South of the United States. I might want to make my comparisons based on regional location using South as my reference point. Thus, comparisons would be made of all other regions to the South. The convention for form is to use the top cells of the table. The extent of the differences between cells are determined by subtracting the column percentage in each of the top cells from the column percentage in the reference cell (e.g. South). Note that the "reference" cell is the most important cell for a particular research project. As a gerontologist you might compare elderly persons to others; As a young person you might select your age group versus others; and so on. What is important to you in presenting the results of your study may differ from what is important to another person.

2 x r table when the independent variable is ordinal

The form in a 2 by r table when n is ordinal is calculated by estimating an average percentage difference across cells. To simplify the overall presentation of results the form is assumed to be uniform (increasing or decreasing equally) as you move across the length of the cross-tab. An ordinal variable may have many categories as we're trying to provide a brief summary of the results rather than force the reader to examine every cell in a table. The form and extent are assessed by taking the column percentage in the top right cell, subtracting the column percentage in the top left cell and dividing by the number of cells that we go across as we move from left to right. The **form** is positive, negative or none. The **extent** is the average percentage difference that results per cell moving across the cross-tab. For example, in a 2 x 3 table we would move across 2 cells. The extent would be the column differences divided by two (3-1=2).

r by c table when r is more than two categories and the independent variable is nominal

Lastly, in an r by c table and when r has more two categories yields several possibilities for assessing form and extent. If r is an ordinal level variable, you should focus on either the top or bottom row of the cross-tab to examine the column percentages as in a nominal level table. If r is nominal with more than 2 categories, you should choose a reference category that is considered as most important to you and report on the column percentages in that row. The objective of cross-tabular analysis is to summarize the most important features of a table rather than to report all of the cell information.

It is critical that you identify the **level of measurement** of each variable and the **number of categories** for each variable so that you may decide how best to determine the form and extent of a bi-variate cross-tabulation.

Statistical Significance of Chi-square

Hypothesis testing in bi-variate tables tests the hypothesis that the two variables are independent of each other. The basic assumptions for the use of chi-square are:

1.   there are independent random samples,
2.   variables are measured at the nominal or ordinal level, and
3.   no expected cell frequency is less than 5.

The null hypothesis is that differences in column percentages are zero (null). The alternative is that the differences are not equal to zero.

We are testing the hypothesis that the chi-square is equal to zero or that the column proportions (percentages) are equal to zero. Essentially, we are looking to see whether the observed frequencies are equal to what would be expected under random conditions of chance. Chi-square is computed as:

$$\chi^2 = \Sigma \frac{(f_o - f_e)^2}{f_e}$$

where f_o = observed cell frequency; and f_e = expected cell frequency. The observed cell frequencies are what you find in your research. The expected cell frequencies are computed as:

$$f_e = \frac{(column\ marginal\ x\ row\ marginal)}{N}$$

The marginals are the totals of the frequencies in each row and column.

To determine if the value of chi-square is significant, we must first determine the degrees of freedom. The degrees of freedom (*df*) is equal to the number of row minus one multiplied by the number of columns minus one. For example, in a 2 x 2 table the *df* is (2-1)(2-1) = 1.

As in the *t* and *F* distributions, χ^2 has a distribution determined by the degrees of freedom. If chi-square exceeds the critical value in the table it is considered as significant. The SPSS computer output prints out an estimate for the probability of obtaining a chi-square of a particular size. If the p-value is less than our alpha level (α=.05 or .01) we will consider the observed value to be significant.

DATA ANALYSIS EXAMPLE

Research Problem: Suppose that we want to find out whether or not high school senior boys are more likely than high school senior girls to have smoked marijuana or hashish in their lifetime. Having tried marijuana or hashish in their lifetime (v115) is the dependent variable and the sex of the students (V150) is the independent variable.

Codebook information:

The Monitoring the Future codebook shows that the question on the survey about marijuana or hashing (V115) in their lifetime is an ordinal level variable with seven categories: None (1), 1-2 time (2), 3-5 times (3), 6-9 times (4) 10-19 (5), 20-39 (6), and 40 or more (7). Think for a moment, why is this considered as an ordinal variable? The answer is that the categories are not the same size (not equidistant). Sex of the student is a nominal level variable with two categories: Male (1), and Female (2).

As in all decision-making tasks, we need to specify our hypothesis. As in most social science problems, we will use an alpha level of $\alpha = .05$.

Null Hypothesis: Lifetime marijuana and hashish use is independent of the sex of the student.
Research Hypothesis: Lifetime marijuana and hashish use is related to the sex of the student.

　　　　To calculate a cross-tabulation you should click on ANALYZE, DESCRIPTIVE STATISTICS, and then select CROSSTABS. The dialogue box follows:

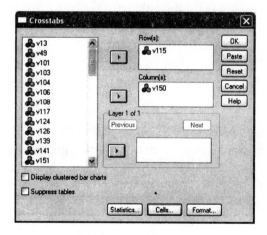

　　　　To obtain the chi-square statistic, click on "Statistics" and check "Chi-square." To obtain column percentages, click on "Cells" and check "Column." By default the frequency count is already checked in the options for cells.

　　　　What will the computer output look like? We know that marijuana and hashish use has seven categories and sex of the student has three categories. We will get a 7 x 2 table with 14 cells. You should make this assessment before calculating the statistics. Making this assessment will also help you to prepare for calculation of form and extent. Notice that missing values are not usually included in calculating the size of a cross-tabulation table.

Computer output:

The case processing summary is important since it will tell us about the number of valid cases in the cross-tabulation. We would like to use variables where fewer than 10 percent of cases are lost. The cross-tab by default removes cases where information is missing on either variable. In our example, we see that about 7 percent of cases are missing. This is an acceptable amount of missing cases.

Case Processing Summary

	Cases					
	Valid		Missing		Total	
	N	Percent	N	Percent	N	Percent
v115 042B07A:#XMJ+ HS/LIFETIME * v150 042C03 :R'S SEX	1396	93.1%	104	6.9%	1500	100.0%

The cross-tab itself is shown on the next page. Note that the independent variable is on top (columns) and the dependent variable is on the side (rows). Since we have only selected column percentages, it is very important that the independent variable be located on top and the dependent variable on the side.

The count and column percent (within sex) are shown. The column percentages each add up to 100 percent.

Reading a cross-tab, it is also useful to double-check that the correct variables have been entered into the table. There are several questions on the Monitoring the Future study that are designed to evaluate drug use. The particular question that we're looking at considers lifetime use of marijuana or hashish. Other questions consider use over the past 30 days and student's attitudes toward the risk of trying it.

v115 042B07A:#XMJ+HS/LIFETIME * v150 042C03 :R'S SEX Crosstabulation

| | | | v150 042C03 :R'S SEX | | |
			1 MALE:(1)	2 FEMALE:(2)	Total
v115 042B07A:#XMJ+ HS/LIFETIME	1 0 OCCAS:(1)	Count	329	428	757
		% within v150 042C03 :R'S SEX	50.0%	58.0%	54.2%
	2 1-2X:(2)	Count	64	80	144
		% within v150 042C03 :R'S SEX	9.7%	10.8%	10.3%
	3 3-5X:(3)	Count	41	44	85
		% within v150 042C03 :R'S SEX	6.2%	6.0%	6.1%
	4 6-9X:(4)	Count	29	42	71
		% within v150 042C03 :R'S SEX	4.4%	5.7%	5.1%
	5 10-19X:(5)	Count	34	42	76
		% within v150 042C03 :R'S SEX	5.2%	5.7%	5.4%
	6 20-39X:(6)	Count	33	30	63
		% within v150 042C03 :R'S SEX	5.0%	4.1%	4.5%
	7 40+OCCAS:(7)	Count	128	72	200
		% within v150 042C03 :R'S SEX	19.5%	9.8%	14.3%
Total		Count	658	738	1396
		% within v150 042C03 :R'S SEX	100.0%	100.0%	100.0%

The computer prints out several kinds of chi-square statistics. We will use the Pearson chi-square statistic.

Chi-Square Tests

	Value	df	Asymp. Sig. (2-sided)
Pearson Chi-Square	29.388[a]	6	.000
Likelihood Ratio	29.557	6	.000
Linear-by-Linear Association	21.531	1	.000
N of Valid Cases	1396		

a. 0 cells (.0%) have expected count less than 5. The minimum expected count is 29.69.

Our analysis shows that there is a significant relationship between lifetime use of marijuana or hashish and sex of the student. The chi-square is 29.4 with 6 *df* and a significance shown as .000. The significance meets our criterion of p<.05. The summary notation is:

153

χ^2 (df) = value, p -value (p< .05; or p> .05),   or χ^2 (6) = 29.4, p<.05

Note that SPSS in this cross-tab reports that there are 0 cells (0.0%) with a low expected count of less than 5. This percentage is calculated as the number of cells with low counts versus the total number of cells (0 of 14 cells; 0.0% of all cells). If this percentage of low cells exceeds 20 percent we would need to consider collapsing categories (recoding variables) or removing some categories. Look back at the cross-tab where you'll see there are smaller cell percentages in the some of the cells in the middle of the table. There are no serious problems for this particular table since 0.0% is less than 20 percent.

Since the relationship between lifetime use of marijuana or hashish and sex of the students is significant, we reject the null hypothesis that there is no relationship between these variables. If a relationship is statistically significant, we proceed to determine the form and extent of the relationship. If we had failed to reject the null hypothesis, we would simply say there is no relationship between the variables.

The form of a 7 x 2 table with a nominal independent variable is calculated by selecting a reference category (By convention, the top right cell) and comparing it to other cells (Top left in this case). The selection of a row is also a matter of convention where the top row is considered. We find that 58.0% of females say that they have not tried marijuana or hashish in their lifetime compared to 50.0% of males. The form of the relationship is that females are more likely than males to say that they have not tried marijuana or hashish. The extent of the relationship is estimated by subtracting the difference as 58.0 – 50.0 = 8.0%. In an overall summary, it is okay to change the focus from "none" to report which sex is more likely to have tried it.

Summary interpretation

The 2004 Monitoring the Future study asked a national sample of high school seniors about their lifetime use of marijuana and hashish using a seven point ordinal scale (none [1], 1-2 [2], 3-5 [3]. 6-9 [4], 10-19 [5], 20-39 [6] and 40 or more times [7]). A chi-squared test can be used to determine if there is a statistical relationship between lifetime marijuana and hashish use and the sex of students (Male [1] and Female [2]). We reject the null hypothesis (χ^2 (6) = 29.4, p<.05). We find that Males are about 8.0 percent more likely than Females to have tried marijuana or hashish with about 50.0 percent of males saying that they had tried one of these drugs.

A good summary of a cross-tabulation will note:

- the source of information
- how the variables were measured
- the decision on chi-square,
- the form and extent of the relationship if chi-square is significant.

KEY TERMS

Cell
Column percentage
Chi-square
Cross-tab
Low expected cell frequency
Non-parametric
Percentage down and compare across
Peason's chi-square
Row percentage
Yate's correction

Web-sites

Sourcebook of Criminal Justice Statistics Online: http://www.albany.edu/sourcebook/

The Sourcebook provides a compilation of about 600 tables on characteristics of the US criminal justice system, public opinion, crime victimization and arrests, the courts, and corrections. For first time users, note that most of these tables report valid percentages and the independent variables will sometimes be presented in rows rather than columns.

Name _____   **Date** _____

1.   *Research Problems:* Use the Monitoring the Future Study to calculate a chi-squared statistic to test the following hypothesis: Male and Female high school seniors will both say that it is easy to get marijuana or hashish (V1780 and V150).

Use the codebook to identify the characteristics of variables.

Write out the null and research hypothesis:

How big will the cross-tab be: (r x c = cells) _____ x _____ = _____

Draw the cross-tab with N's and column percentages:

Statistics(Chi-square)

Write a summary interpretation

Name _____   **Date** _____

2.   *Research Problems:* Use the Monitoring the Future Study to calculate a chi-squared statistic to test the following hypothesis: lifetime cocaine use (V124) will differ by sex (V150).

Use the codebook to identify the characteristics of variables.

Write out the null and research hypothesis:

How big will the cross-tab be: (r x c = cells) _____ x _____ = _____

Draw the cross-tab with N's and column percentages:

Statistics(Chi-square)

Write a summary interpretation

Name _____   **Date** _____

3.   *Research Problems:* Use the Monitoring the Future Study to calculate a chi-squared statistic to test the following hypothesis: Lifetime marijuana or hashish use (V115) will differ by regional location (V13).

Use the codebook to identify the characteristics of variables.

Write out the null and research hypothesis:

How big will the cross-tab be: (r x c = cells) _____ x _____ = _____

Draw the cross-tab with N's and column percentages:

Statistics(Chi-square)

Write a summary interpretation

Name _____   **Date** _____

4.   *Research Problems:* Use the General Social Survey to calculate a chi-squared statistic to test the following hypothesis: Older persons are more likely than younger persons to fear crime (fear and age).

Use the codebook to identify the characteristics of variables.

Write out your hypothesis:

How big will the crosstab be: (r x c = cells) _____ x _____ = _____

(Remember that age goes from 18 through 89)

Use SPSS to calculate chi-squared.

What is the percentage of cells with low expected frequency counts? _____

Is this an acceptable percentage? Yes / No Explain.

Is this table easy to read? Yes / No

What could be done to improve it? Explain.

Name _____   **Date** _____

5.   Using methods that you learned in chapter 3, recode age into 3 or 4 age groups (e.g. 18 to 29; 30 to 54; 55 to 89). Recalculate chi-squared using the recoded variable.

Write out your hypothesis?

How big will the new cross-tab be: _____ x _____ = _____

Draw the new cross-tab with N's and column percentages

Statistics(Chi-square)

Write a summary interpretation

Name _____   **Date** _____

6.   *Research Problem:*

Choose two variables from any of the data sets.

Use the codebook to identify the characteristics of all variables.

Write out your hypothesis:

How big will the cross-tab be: (r x c = cells) _____ x _____ = _____

Draw the cross-tab with N's and column percentages:

Statistics(Chi-square)

Write a summary interpretation

Name _____   **Date** _____

7.   *Research Problem:*

Use your college library to find two articles on attitudes toward abortion.

Use the General Social Survey to calculate chi-squared statistics to test hypotheses for each of the abortion variables (Abany, abrape, absingle) cross-tabulated by several variables of your choice.

What kinds of variables do you think will be related to public opinion about abortion?

Write out one of your hypotheses here

Draw the cross-tab

Statistics

Continue on with additional tests. Write a four to six page paper summarizing the results of your research.

Name _____   **Date** _____

Use Fox's Statistics Calculator to calculate a two-way chi-square test.

8.   *Research Problem:*

Is there a sex difference in red-light running? A researcher completes an exploratory observational study at a major intersection in Crash City, USA. Observations are made watching cars from when the point where the light turns from green (GO) to yellow (Caution), and then yellow to Red (Stop). Traffic violations and sex of the driver are recorded.

	Sex	
Action	**Male**	**Female**
Runs red	21	10
Runs yellow	23	22
Slows and stops	55	76

a.   Write out the null hypothesis

b.   Write out the research hypothesis

c.   What are the degrees of freedom? _____

d.   Assuming an alpha of .05, what is the critical value of chi-square? _____

e.   Assuming an alpha of .01, what is the critical value of chi-square? _____

f.   What is the chi-square? _____

g.   What is the statistical conclusion for both levels of alpha?

Name _____ Date _____

Use Fox's Statistics Calculator to calculate a two-way chi-square test.

Research Problem:

9. Medical evidence shows that breast-feeding has long-term health benefits for both the mother and the child. Nonetheless, many American mothers choose not to breastfeed because of the social stigma against breastfeeding in public. Some persons argue that hospitals make it too easy for women to choose formula because they provide infant formula samples at the hospital. What does the general public think about this issue? A researcher completes a telephone survey asking parents and non-parents about providing formula.

	Has children?	
Action	**Parent**	**Non-parent**
Give infant formula to ALL new mothers	293	107
Give infant formula ONLY to new mothers that cannot breastfeed	90	37

a. Write out the null hypothesis

b. Write out the research hypothesis

c. What are the degrees of freedom? _____

d. Assuming an alpha of .05, what is the critical value of chi-square? _____

e. Assuming an alpha of .01, what is the critical value of chi-square? _____

f. What is the chi-square? _____

g. What is the statistical conclusion for both levels of alpha?

CORRELATION

INTRODUCTION

Correlation is introduced as a powerful technique for analyzing the linear relationship between two variables that are measured at the *interval* or *ratio* levels, and in a special case with two category nominal level variables. In this chapter, you will be introduced to correlation and its most popular version: Pearson's correlation (r). You will see that correlation tests the degree of association of variables allowing an interpretation of the form, extent and precision of bi-variate relationships.

SCATTERPLOTS

In a cross-tabulation the variables need to be discrete so that we can fit them into a cell within the table. Correlational analysis is a more powerful procedure because unlike cross-tabs we can work with variables with many categories and with continuous metrics. A scatterplot allows us to examine the joint distribution and a correlation allows us to describe the relationship between the variables.

A scatterplot is a plot of the position of each observation with the independent variable on the horizontal axis and the dependent variable on the vertical axis. The closer that the cases bunch together like a thin line, the stronger the association. Using a scatterplot, we may obtain a graphical presentation of the form, extent, and precision of relationships of variables measured at the interval and ratio level.

FORM OF RELATIONSHIPS IN SCATTERPLOTS

Let's look at some hypothetical data to illustrate different forms of relationships. Figure 1 shows a linear and a curvilinear relationship between seriousness of offense and length of sentence. Note that each point on the scatterplot represents a single person's score on each variable. A linear relationship will look like a straight line. A curvilinear relationship may take on many different forms. A scatterplot allows a quick check on the form. Note that most correlation coefficients assume that there is a linear relationship between variables. A scatterplot simply allows a visual test of the form of the relationship. In this chapter, we will take the conventional assumption that all of the relationships are linear.

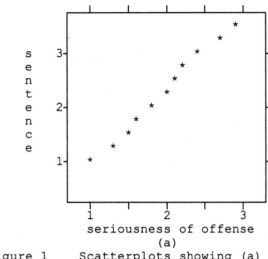
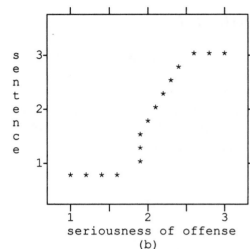

Figure 1   Scatterplots showing (a) a linear, and (b) a curvilinear
relationship.

EXTENT OF RELATIONSHIPS IN SCATTERPLOTS

Moving to Figure 2, there are three scatterplots hypothetically illustrating the extent of association between the length of a prison sentence in relation to seriousness of offense. The extent of a correlation is positive if the joint values on the dependent variable increase as values on the independent variable increase. A negative correlation suggests that values on the independent variable increase the joint values on the dependent variable decrease. If there is no correlation between the variables the scores will appear to be randomly distributed throughout the scatterplot.

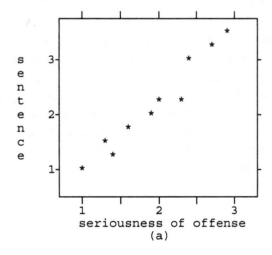
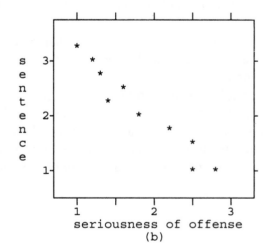

PEARSON'S CORRELATION COEFFICIENT: *r*

Scatterplots provide a visual aid. We turn now to the numerical calculation of Pearson's correlation coefficient. With it we may determine the extent and precision of relationship between variables. The form is assumed to be linear. The formula for Pearson's correlation is:

$$r = \frac{\Sigma(X - \overline{X})(Y - \overline{Y})}{\sqrt{\Sigma(X - \overline{X})^2 \, \Sigma(Y - \overline{Y})^2}}$$

The numerator is called the covariance of Y and X, where X and Y are the joint values on a variable for a case in comparison to the means of X and Y. The denominator is similar to a standard deviation of each variable. Thus, r is defined as the ratio of the product of the standard deviations of Y and X to the covariance of Y and X.

Form

The form of the relationship of Pearson's *r* refers to the direction of a correlation which may be positive (direct), negative (inverse), or null (zero).

Extent

The extent of *r* refers to the magnitude or strength of the correlation. The extent ranges in magnitude from -1 to +1. For Pearson's *r* we use a benchmark for the extent of the relationship: 0 to .1 is weak; .1 to .3 is weak to moderate; .3 to .6 is moderate to strong; .6 to 1 is very strong to perfect. Zero indicates no relationship between the variables. The further that *r* is from zero, the stronger the relationship.

Level of significance

The level of significance of *r* is calculated by converting it to a t score. The formula is:

$$t = r \sqrt{\frac{N - 2}{1 - r^2}}$$

Where *r* = the calculated correlation coefficient; and N = the sample size.

DATA ANALYSIS EXAMPLE

Research Problem: Using the General Social Survey, what are the statistical relationships between sex (SEX), socioeconomic index (SEI), and attitudes toward governmental assistance in helping the poor (HELPPOOR) and the sick (HELPSICK).

Codebook information: Use the codebook to get basic information about each variable.

Helping the poor is a scale ranging from 1 to 5 operationalized as government should help (1) to people should help themselves (5). We will assume that this is an interval level variable with a metric of 1 unit of helping.

Helping the sick is measured on the same scale as helping the poor.

Socioeconomic index is measured at a continuous scalar variable ranging from 17.1 to 97.2 (higher numbers indicated higher status).

Sex of the respondent is a two category nominal level variable measured as male (1) or female (2). Two-category nominal level variables can be entered into correlation as a special case. In chapter 12, you will see another way to test this relationship.

Hypotheses:

Write out a null and research hypothesis for each problem. You must specify hypotheses for each pairs of variables that you wish to test. Use $\alpha = .05$

Null Hypothesis: $r = 0$
Attitudes toward helping the sick are not related to people's socioeconomic status.
Research Hypothesis: $r \neq 0$
Attitudes toward helping the sick are related to people's socioeconomic status.

Null Hypothesis: $r = 0$
Attitudes toward helping the poor are not related to attitudes toward helping the sick.
Research Hypothesis: $r \neq 0$
People attitudes toward the poor are related to their attitudes toward helping the sick.

Null Hypothesis: $r = 0$
Sex is independent of attitudes toward helping the sick.
Research Hypothesis: $r \neq 0$
Females will differ from males in attitudes toward helping the sick.

Note that you may develop as many hypotheses as there are pairs of variables. You do not have to have a hypothesis for every pair. Hypotheses are only necessary for pairs where you wish to test a relationship. Here we will only examine three pairs.

There are several ways to obtain correlations in SPSS. We will use the correlations procedure to obtain a *correlation matrix* requesting information on the correlation, the sample size, and the probability value based on a two-tailed level of significance. The procedure is obtained though ANALYZE, CORRELATE, and BIVARIATE. The dialogue box is shown below:

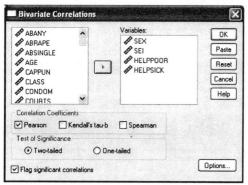

All of the variables are entered (in any order) into the same analysis. We select the Pearson correlation and two-tailed tests of significance. SPSS, by default, will "flag" correlations that are significant at the .05 and .01 levels. It also prints the significance level. SPSS reports N's for each correlation as the number of cases where both elements are valid (e.g. a person answers both questions on a survey).

Computer output:

Correlations

		SEX RESPONDENTS SEX	SEI RESPONDENT SOCIOECONOMIC INDEX	HELPPOOR SHOULD GOVT IMPROVE STANDARD OF LIVING?	HELPSICK SHOULD GOVT HELP PAY FOR MEDICAL CARE?
SEX RESPONDENTS SEX	Pearson Correlation	1	-.045	-.072	-.130**
	Sig. (2-tailed)		.089	.122	.005
	N	1500	1409	462	461
SEI RESPONDENT SOCIOECONOMIC INDEX	Pearson Correlation	-.045	1	.058	.022
	Sig. (2-tailed)	.089		.236	.646
	N	1409	1409	424	422
HELPPOOR SHOULD GOVT IMPROVE STANDARD OF LIVING?	Pearson Correlation	-.072	.058	1	.464**
	Sig. (2-tailed)	.122	.236		.000
	N	462	424	462	457
HELPSICK SHOULD GOVT HELP PAY FOR MEDICAL CARE?	Pearson Correlation	-.130**	.022	.464**	1
	Sig. (2-tailed)	.005	.646	.000	
	N	461	422	457	461

** Correlation is significant at the 0.01 level (2-tailed).

Let's look at the correlation matrix. Note the "1" for the correlation of Sex with sex, SEI with SEI, and so on. These 1's allow an easy identification of the diagonal of the matrix. The significance of these correlations is not shown (printed as a dot in SPSS 13.0) which means it is not applicable. The N's here tell us the number of people who answered each particular question. So, 1500 people gave us a valid answer about their sex. How many people told us information about their socioeconomic index? What they think about government helping the poor? And, helping the sick? The N's are shown each diagonal box as 1409, 462, and 461. Why are the N's for helping the poor and helping the sick soc much lower than the N's for sex and SEI? Remember that these attitudinal questions were not asked of everyone on the survey while demographic and economic questions were asked of everyone.

The correlations on either side of the diagonal (identity matrix) are symmetrical. Look at the correlation of sex with helping the poor in column 1 and row 3 (r=-.072). It is the same value as the correlation of help the poor with sex (r=-.072) in column 3 and row 1. We can locate the correlation of two variables on either side of the diagonal. The APA manual recommends that only the top half of the correlation matrix be presented in a summary table.

The general form for expressing a correlation is shown below:

General form: r = value, p-level (p<.05, or p>.05).

Interpretation of correlation coefficients:

The computer will print out r and a two-tailed probability for estimating its significance. We will use an alpha level of α = .05 to test the hypotheses.

Testing hypothesis 1, we find a positive correlation between socioeconomic index and attitudes toward helping the sick. Find the r= .022 in the matrix. To test its significance we simply read the significance value from the matrix as p=.646 and assess whether it is below our alpha level of .05. It is not and hence it fails to meet our criterion for significance. We fail to reject the null hypothesis and conclude that there is no statistical relationship between these variables (r=.022, p>.05).

Testing hypothesis 2, we find a correlation of +.464 between attitudes toward helping the sick and attitudes toward helping the poor. The computer output shows p =.000. This value is clearly below our alpha level of .05. Find the values of r= .464 and Sig = .000 in the matrix. We reject the null hypothesis (r = .464, p<.05.) We may calculate form and extent when there is a relationship between variables. The form is positive and the extent is between .3 and .6 which is an indication of a moderately strong correlation.

The actual scatterplot of attitudes toward helping the sick by attitudes toward helping the poor is shown below. Quite clearly the distribution of scores doesn't look much like a positive relationship. Unlike the idealized plots shown at the beginning of this chapter, it is often difficult to see graphically whether there is a relationship between variables with only a few categories.

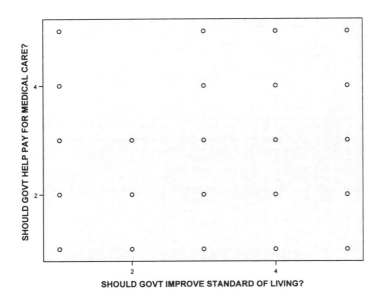

Testing hypothesis 3, we find a negative relationship between sex and attitudes toward helping the sick. Find r=-130 in the computer output. Is -.130 significant? We look at the computer output to find .005. This is below our alpha level so that we reject the null hypothesis. The form of the relationship is that women are more likely than men to say that the government should help the sick. The extent of the correlation is between .1 and .3 indicating a weak correlation (r=-.13, p<.05).

Summary Interpretation

The 2004 General Social Survey queried Americans about some of their attitudes toward governmental assistance in helping the poor and helping the sick. For example, people were asked whether or not the government should help people who are sick in paying for their medical care. The question on helping was measured using a five point scale ranging from the government should help (1) to people should help themselves (5). A correlational analysis was used to determine whether people's socioeconomic index and sex are related to attitudes toward helping the sick. Additionally, a question on whether or not attitudes toward governmental assistance for the poor was examined. The alpha level for these tests was set at .05. The results of these tests suggest socioeconomic status is not related to attitudes toward helping the sick

(r=.022, p>.05). There is a weak correlation between sex and attitudes toward helping the sick as women are more likely than men to agree that the government should help the sick (r=-.13, p<.05). And, there is a moderately strong relationship between attitudes toward helping the sick and attitudes toward helping the poor (r=.46, p<.05).

When writing up a correlational analysis:

- State the source of information
- Describe the measurement of each of the variables.
- Indicate the level of confidence
- State the decision on the null hypothesis as reject or fail to reject
- If significant, calculate form and extent
- Use a table if there are a large number of variables in an analysis. APA format suggests reporting the top half of the matrix.
- If only a few correlation statistics are reported they can be done in the text of a summary.

KEY TERMS

Correlation
Correlation matrix
Pearson's r (note the italics)
Diagonal of matrix
Inverse (negative)
Direct (positive)
Linear correlation
Scatterplot

Name _____   **Date** _____

1.   Research Problems: Use the General Social Survey to calculate Pearson's *r* to test the
following hypotheses:

Research hypothesis 1.   Respondent's socioeconomic index (SEI) is related to their
personal income (RINCOM98).

Research hypothesis 2.   Higher levels of education (Degree) are directly related to higher
socioeconomic index scores (SEI).

Research hypothesis 3.   Males will have higher personal income than females (Rincom98
and Sex).

Research hypothesis 4.   Add a pair of variables of your own selection. You may pair one
of the above variables with one additional variable.

Use the codebook to identify the characteristics of variables.

Write out the null and research hypotheses

Record the correlation matrix for these variables (Pearson's *r)*.

Interpret the results

Name _____   **Date** _____

2.   *Research Problems:* Use the Monitoring the Future Study to calculate Pearson's *r* to test the following hypotheses:

Research hypothesis 1.   Lifetime reported use of marijuana or hashish (V115) and lifetime reported use of cocaine (V124).

Research hypothesis 2.   Students who use marijuana or hashish (V115) are more likely to get speeding tickets V197).

Research hypothesis 3.   Add a pair of variables of your own selection. You may pair one of the above variables with one additional variable.

Use the codebook to identify the characteristics of variables.

Write out the null and research hypotheses

Name _____   **Date** _____

Record the correlation matrix for these variables (Pearson's *r)*.

Interpret the results

Name _____   Date _____

3.   *Research Problems:* Use the General Social Survey to calculate Pearson's *r* to test hypotheses about relationships between time out socializing (bar, friends, relatives), sex of the respondent, age, and television viewing habits.

Write out your hypotheses:

Use the codebook to identify the characteristics of variables.

Name _____   **Date** _____

Record the correlation matrix for these variables (Pearson's *r)*.

Interpret the results

Name _____   **Date** _____

4.   Use your college library to find two articles on public attitudes toward "legalization of marijuana" and demographic factors.

Identify two or more variables in the Monitoring the Future Study that would allow a test of this relationship.

Identify two or more variables in the General Social Study that would allow a test of this relationship.

5.   Use Fox's Statistics Calculator to calculate Pearson's r.

A researcher was interested in determining the degree of association between unemployment rate (X) and the crime rate (Y). She found the information for the 9 largest cities in her region of the county. The results were:

Subject	Unemployment %	Homicide rate per 100,000
A	6.1	20.2
B	2.2	5.3
C	5.5	8.1
D	5.1	9.0
E	7.9	30.5
F	4.3	5.1
G	5.5	7.0
H	6.2	11.5
I	5.2	8.2

a.   What is Pearson's r? _____

b.   What is the critical value of r, assuming a value of .01? _____

c.   What is the critical value of r, assuming a value of .05? _____

d.   Is the correlation between unemployment and the murder rate significant at the .01 level?

e.   Is it significant at the .05 level?

f.   If appropriate, interpret the form and extent

REGRESSION ANALYSIS

INTRODUCTION

Regression analysis is one of the most powerful methods for analyzing linear relationships between two variables measured at the interval or ratio levels. Essentially, regression analysis may be used to identify an **association** between variables and to use this information to make **predictions** about the value of a dependent variable from one or more independent variables.

Correlation analysis is used to inform us about the accuracy of predictions from regression and to describe the nature of the relationship. This chapter introduces you to regression analysis by having you work with examples using two variables that are assumed to be linearly related to each other. We will interpret the form, extent and precision of these relationships.

REGRESSION MODEL

Let's begin with some hypothetical data on sentencing and the seriousness of the crime. Sentence length is operationalized as time in years. Seriousness of the crime is a scale going from not at all serious (0) to extremely serious (10). A researcher examines ten cases selected at random from her local court:

Case	Sentence	Seriousness of crime
1	12	3
2	20	10
3	25	10
4	3	1
5	4	1
6	3	2
7	15	7
8	18	6
9	1	1
10	2	2

Regression analysis allows us to see whether or not there is a relationship between the length of a sentence and the seriousness of a crime. A scatterplot is shown on the next page.

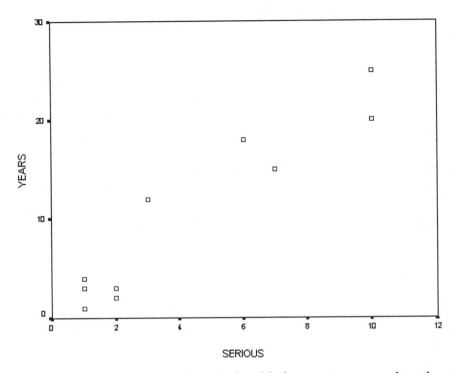

SERIOUS

It appears to the eye that there is a relationship between sentence length and seriousness of the offense. Regression analysis assumes that there is a linear relationship between variables. Where would we draw a straight line on the above scatterplot? Regression analysis will tell us where to draw the line so that we can minimize the errors in our estimate for a predicted value.

Levin and Fox, in Chapter 11, provide a discussion of the foundations of regression. The formula for the regression line is shown below:

$$Y = a + b\,X + e$$

The relationship between variables is assumed to be linear approximated by a straight line with a slope (b) and an intercept (a). The slope of a line is defined as the vertical distance divided by the horizontal distance between any two points on the regression line. The intercept is the point where the regression line intersects with the y-axis (where x = zero). We use the term "e" to represent the residual (or error) in predicting y from x.

The regression line is drawn on to the figure on the next page using the coordinates (X, Y) for the intercept (0, .50) and the means of X and Y (4.3, 10.3).

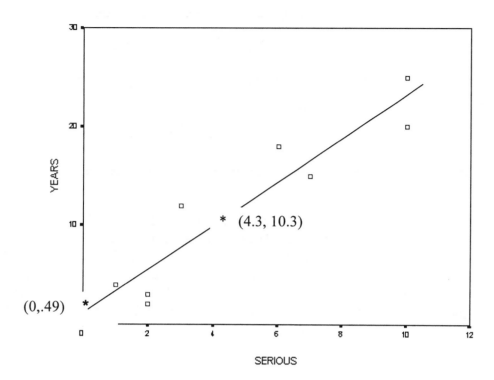

Notice that some of the scores fall below the line while others are above it. The regression line is the best guess for the relationship between the variables. The regression procedure will tell how well we are able to do in our estimates. Have a look back at Levin and Fox's chapter to see how the intercept and slope are calculated. Here in the workbook, we're going to look at the computer output and go beyond it to show how regression analysis can be used to make predictions.

In regression analysis, a mathematical equation is used to predict the value of the dependent variable ($\hat{Y}$) for a given a value of the independent variable (X).

$$\hat{Y} = a + bX$$

When we find a significant relationship between variables, we can use the regression line to predict values of the dependent variable for expressed values of an independent variable. A regression analysis of seriousness on sentencing yields an intercept of .48 and a slope of 2.28. The table on the next page shows the expected (predicted) sentence length for crimes with seriousness of 1, 5, and 8. Using a regression equation, we predict that people who commit crimes of serious "1" are expected to get a sentence of 2.77 years in prison.

$\hat{Y}= a + b X$ predicting sentence length based on crime seriousness			
$\hat{Y}$	a	b	X
2.77	0.49	2.28	1
11.89	0.49	2.28	5
18.73	0.49	2.28	8

The regression line for $\hat{Y}$ is a best guess for a predicted value. Most cases in a regression analysis will fall above or below the regression line. The difference between the best guess and the actual value for a case is called a residual (or error) in predicting Y from X. For these hypothetical data, regression analysis provides a PRE statistic (R-squared) suggesting that there is a very strong relationship between these variables so that we will be correct 89 percent of the time. Let's go to the computer output using some real data to illustrate the steps to interpret a regression model.

Form

In regression we will assume that relationships between variables are linear. There are other types of non-linear regression models but they fall outside the scope of an introductory course.

Extent

In regression, we may examine two aspects of the extent of relationships: unstandardized and standardized. The extent of relationships refers to the slope of a regression line. The slope is conceptualized as the number of units that the y variable will increase given a value of X. The unstandardized slope (beta or b) use the original metrics of Y and X. The standardized slope (BETA or B) is identical to correlation in bivariate regression where the standard deviations of both variables are used to estimate the slope of the regression line.

The magnitude of the extent of the slope of an unstandardized regression line will depend on the attributes of the variables that are being examined (e.g. dollars, crimes, behaviors, etc.). The extent of BETA ranges from -1 to +1, and the extent refers to whether the sign is positive (direct) or negative (inverse) and its magnitude.

Level of significance of the regression model

To determine the significance of a regression model, you should notice that there are strong similarities between regression and analysis of variance. ANOVA broke the total sum of squares into between and within group sum of squares. In regression, a researcher will want to know whether an independent variable is able to explain variation in a dependent variable. Fortunately, you'll see that an analysis of variance table is a concise way of presenting the results of a regression analysis.

Precision

The precision of a regression line is estimated by using the squared correlation coefficient which is also called the coefficient of determination. A larger value of r^2 indicates a stronger fit of scores around the regression line. The complementary quantity of $1 - r^2$ is called the coefficient of non-determination. It represents the proportion of variance in Y this is not explained by X. Multiple regression is an extension of simple bivariate regression. It uses a multiple coefficient of determination R^2 and an adjusted R^2 which takes into account the number of independent variables in the equation. This multiple coefficient of determination is the proportion of variance in a dependent variable that is explained by a set of independent variables.

DATA ANALYSIS EXAMPLE

Research Problem: Is lifetime cocaine use (v124) related to lifetime marijuana and hashish use (v115) among high school students?

We will use regression analysis to examine this issue using a sample of High School Students from the 2004 Monitoring the Future Study.

Codebook information: Use the codebook to get basic information about each variable.

The lifetime use of cocaine and the lifetime use of marijuana or hashish are both measured using a "normalized scale" 1 "0 occassions" to 7 "40 or more times." We will treat these variables as if they were interval level scales with a known metric of 1 unit of use. We will use an $\alpha = .05$.

The regression procedure is accessed by clicking on ANALYZE, REGRESSION, and then LINEAR. Move the dependent and independent variables into their respective boxes. We will use the default method to "enter" the variables into the regression model. You can also check the "descriptives" in the "Statistics" box to get the means for the two variables.

The dialogue box follows:

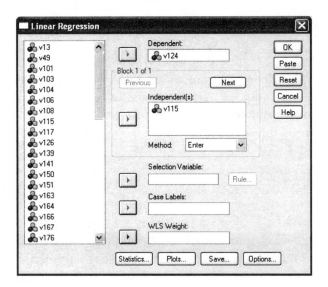

Computer output:

A large amount of information is produced in the regression output with many features that you will not need for bi-variate regression. You will have to look in the output for the appropriate bi-variate regression statistics. Most programs provide a model summary, an ANOVA test, and the regression coefficients.

The ANOVA test tells us whether there is a statistical relationship between the dependent variable and the predictor variable(s).

ANOVA[b]

Model		Sum of Squares	df	Mean Square	F	Sig.
1	Regression	182.932	1	182.932	257.593	.000[a]
	Residual	1013.398	1427	.710		
	Total	1196.330	1428			

a. Predictors: (Constant), v115 042B07A:#XMJ+HS/LIFETIME

b. Dependent Variable: v124 042B10A:#X COKE/LIFETIME

In this case, the F-ratio is significant (F=257.6, p<.05). Since it is significant we will determine the regression line.

Regression procedures generate more information than is required leaving it up to the reader to extract the information that he or she needs. The "coefficients" table provides the intercept (a) and slope (b) listed as unstandardized coefficients. The other statistics in this table go beyond the scope of Levin and Fox's textbook and this workbook.

Coefficients[a]

Model		Unstandardized Coefficients		Standardized Coefficients		
		B	Std. Error	Beta	t	Sig.
1	(Constant)	.808	.035		23.362	.000
	v115 042B07A:#XMJ+ HS/LIFETIME	.158	.010	.391	16.050	.000

a. Dependent Variable: v124 042B10A:#X COKE/LIFETIME

Let's locate the pertinent information in the above table for a regression equation predicting cocaine use. Recall that the predicted value is:

$$\hat{Y} = a + b\,X$$

The intercept (a) is called a "Constant" in the SPSS computer output. We substitute the unstandardized coefficients for the intercept and the slope into the equation to obtain:

$$\hat{Y} = .808 + .158\,X$$

The slope suggests that for each one unit increase in marijuana and hashish use that cocaine use increases by .158 units.

The coefficient of determination (precision) can be read directly from the computer output in the model summary. It is symbolized by an r^2 because Pearson's r^2 in correlation is connected to regression with two variables. In this example, it represents the proportion of variance in the dependent variable given one independent variable.

Model Summary

Model	R	R Square	Adjusted R Square	Std. Error of the Estimate
1	.391[a]	.153	.152	.843

a. Predictors: (Constant), v115 042B07A:#XMJ+HS/LIFETIME

The model summary shows that a modest amount of the variance in cocaine use is explained when we know about marijuana and hashish use. The coefficient of determination $r^2 = .153$. The coefficient of non-determination $1 - r^2 = .847$. That is, we can explain about 15% of the variance in cocaine use when we know about marijuana and hashish use.

Interpretation

We will interpret the features of the regression line: form and precision. We will also use the regression line to predicted value for a student that has used marijuana or hashish 3-5 times (3). Note that we will use an alpha level of $\alpha = .05$ to test our hypothesis.

The form of all regression lines is assumed to be linear. Keep this in mind as we make our interpretation.

In testing the hypothesis, we look to the t-value testing the slope for the independent variable. We found a significant slope based on $F=257.6, p<.05$.

Regression is a more powerful tool than correlation. When we reject the find a significant relationship we can use the unstandardized values to make predictions about our dependent variable. Our predicted value ($\hat{Y}$) can be estimated using information from the table.

$$\hat{Y} = a + b\,X$$

a is the intercept or constant
b is the unstandardized slope; and
X is the value we wish to insert for the independent variable

In our example, we insert the information from the regression table to get

$\hat{Y} = 0.808 + .158\,(3)$
$\hat{y} = 1.282$ which rounds to a whole number of 1

A 1 on the 1 to 7 scale corresponds with a predicted value of having never tried cocaine in the student's lifetime.

The precision of the relationship is weak ($r^2 = .153$; rounded as $r^2 = .15$). We find that we are able to explain about 15 percent of the variation in reported lifetime cocaine use when we know about a student's lifetime marijuana or hashish use.

In bi-variate regression, we can also draw a regression line on a scatterplot. Look back at the codebook for the values for each variable. On the y-axis, draw out cocaine use on the y-axis and marijuana or hashish use on its 1 to 7 scale on the x-axis. Extend each of these scales past their ends so that they include a 0. From the coefficients for the regression model we have information about the intercept shown as the constant. Draw the intercept following (X, Y) as (0, 0.8).

To locate the regression line we're going to need the means. These were obtained by checking descriptions in the options box for the regression procedure.

Descriptive Statistics

	Mean	Std. Deviation	N
v124 042B10A:#X COKE/LIFETIME	1.23	.915	1429
v115 042B07A:#XMJ+ HS/LIFETIME	2.68	2.264	1429

The means for cocaine and marijuana / hashish are (2.7, 1.2). Locate this on scatterplot, join the dots and you'll have a regression line predicting lifetime cocaine use based on lifetime marijuana or hashish use.

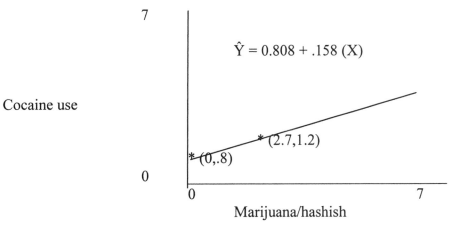

We have covered a lot of ground with regression and shown you some of how it is connected with ANOVA and correlation. A summary interpretation of a regression model should report:

- source of information
- whether there is a significant relationship between variables
- a summary table of the regression coefficients
- the coefficient of determination
- some key predictions to answer the researcher's most important issues

KEY TERMS

Adjusted R^2
Beta
Coefficient of determination
Coefficient of non-determination
F-Ratio
Intercept
Linear regression
Model summary
Predicted value
Regression
Slope
r^2
R^2
Unstandardized beta

Name _____   **Date** _____

Research Problems: Use linear regression to test the following hypothesis:

1.   From the GSS, there is a relationship between respondent's income (Rincom98) and their socioeconomic index (SEI).

Use the codebook to identify the characteristics of variables.

Write out the null and research hypotheses

Calculate the regression model

What is the predicted value of income for one category of education?

Interpret the results

Name _____   **Date** _____

Research Problems: Use linear regression to test the following hypothesis:

2.   From the MTF study, high school seniors that skip classes (V176) are more likely to have smoked marijuana or hashish in their lifetime (V115).

Use the codebook to identify the characteristics of variables.

Write out the null and research hypotheses

Calculate the regression model

What is the predicted amount of marijuana or hashish use for:

Someone who has never skipped classes _____

Someone who has skipped 23 days (_____ on the scale) _____

Interpret the results

Use your college library to find two articles on truancy and drug use. Compare your findings with their work.

Research Problems: Use linear regression to test a hypothesis:

3.   Choose two variables from any data set.

Use the codebook to identify the characteristics of variables.

Write out the null and research hypotheses

Calculate the regression model

Make a prediction for one value of the independent variable:

Draw a scatterplot and draw the regression line using the intercept and means.

Name _____   **Date** _____

Use Fox's Statistics Calculator to conduct a regression analysis of the following:

4.   A research has gathered data from seven randomly selected employees on the number of years (X) employees have worked in a particular department and their salaries (Y) in thousands of dollars.

No. Years (X)	Salaries (Y)
1	25.5
2	27.0
2	27.25
4	28.5
5	33
7	33
7	34.5

a.   What is the slope of the regression line? _____

b.   What is the intercept of the regression line? _____

c.   Using the F-ratio, are these results significant at the .01 level?

d.   What would the predicted salary be for someone in the department who has worked 6 years? _____

e.   What is the prediction error for someone who has worked in the department for 6 years?

NONPARAMETRIC MEASURES OF CORRELATION

INTRODUCTION

In this chapter, we will look at some examples where alternative non-parametric measures are necessary because the assumptions required for Pearson's r are not met. Specicically, nonparametric measures are used when nominal or ordinal variables must be used or there is non-normality in the population.

This lab introduces you to Spearman's rank-order correlation coefficient, Goodman and Kruskal's gamma, phi coefficient, contingency coefficient, and Cramér's V.

RANK-ORDER CORRELATION

The rank order correlation assumes:
- A straight line (linear) correlation
- Ordinal data
- And, random sampling

The interpretation is very similar to what we did in chapter 10 with Pearson's *r*. We will often use Spearman's rank order correlation when we're not comfortable making an assumption that a rank-order variable is truly an interval level variable.

For example, lifetime use of marijuana or hashish is an ordinal scale ranging from never (1) to 40 or more time (7), and lifetime use of cocaine is measured on the same ordinal scale.

In this instance we can make the argument that marijuana or hashish use is expected to be linearly correlated with cocaine use. We're not saying that use will be at the same degree but we are testing whether there is a linear relationship between the variables. Both variables are measured at the ordinal variable. The Monitoring the Future Study also uses random sampling. Thus, we can calculate the rank ordered correlation.

To obtain a Spearman's correlation, click on ANALYZE, CORRELATE, BIVARIATE, and then check Spearman's and unclick Pearson's. The box is shown on the next page:

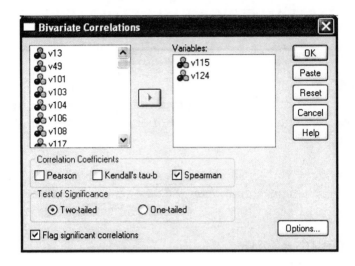

The results look very similar to Pearson's correlation. The correlation, significance, and N's are shown.

Correlations

			v115 042B07A:# XMJ+HS/ LIFETIME	v124 042B10A:#X COKE/ LIFETIME
Spearman's rho	v115 042B07A:#XMJ+ HS/LIFETIME	Correlation Coefficient	1.000	.414**
		Sig. (2-tailed)	.	.000
		N	1439	1429
	v124 042B10A:#X COKE/LIFETIME	Correlation Coefficient	.414**	1.000
		Sig. (2-tailed)	.000	.
		N	1429	1456

**. Correlation is significant at the 0.01 level (2-tailed).

The form and extent are interpreted very much as you would interpret a Pearson's correlation. Here the Spearman's correlation falling between .3 and .6 indicates a moderately strong correlation (look back at strength of relationships in Chapter 10, page 167) between use of marijuana or hashish and use of cocaine. The r_s = .414, p <.01.

GOODMAN AND KRUSKAL'S GAMMA

A second nonparametric measure is Goodman and Kruskal's Gamma. It is particularly useful for assessing association when two ordinal variables are cross-tabulated. It assumes:
- Two variables measured at the ordinal level
- Random sampling

Unlike Spearman's rank order correlation, it doe not require a linear relationship. It's interpretation is also very similar to Pearson's *r*.

Using the General Social Survey, let's examine how often people go out at night to visit friends and how often they go out to bars. Both variables are clearly ranked ranging from Almost daily (1) through never (7). The GSS used random sampling.

In using gamma, we can estimate the degree of association between these variables without having to stretch assumptions on whether these are interval level variables, and we also don't have to worry about problems of normality.

To obtain gamma, use the cross-tabs procedure placing the variables (SOCBAR and SOCFREND) in the crosstabs box, and check "Gamma" in the Statistics box:

How large will the cross-tabs table be? The answer is 7 x 7 or 49 cells. A giant! Fortunately, we're not interested in the table as we only need the Gamma statistic.

The statistics are printed at the end of the crosstabulation. The Gamma is G=.347 and it is significant at the .05 level. G=.325, p<.05.

Symmetric Measures

		Value	Asymp. Std. Error[a]	Approx. T[b]	Approx. Sig.
Ordinal by Ordinal	Gamma	.347	.045	7.421	.000
N of Valid Cases		468			

a. Not assuming the null hypothesis.

b. Using the asymptotic standard error assuming the null hypothesis.

The Gamma is interpreted using the same benchmark that we used with Pearson's *r* so that we have found a moderate relationship between nights out going to the bar and nights out going to visit friends.

2 x 2 TABLES WITH NOMINAL DATA

The phi coefficient is used when nominal data can be arranged in a 2 x 2 table. It is easily obtained since it is an extension of the chi-square test. It provides a simple estimate of the correlation.

Phi (ϕ) is calculated as a derivative of chi-squared (χ^2) and sample size (N):

$$\phi = \sqrt{\frac{\chi^2}{N}}$$

For example, the GSS measures attitudes toward the death penalty by asking respondents whether they favor (1) or oppose (2) the death penalty for murder. Let's see whether this is correlated with a person's sex categorized as male (1) and female (2). Thus, we have a 2 x 2 table with the counts for each cell shown below:

Attitudes toward the death penalty for murder by sex

Count

		SEX		
		1 MALE	2 FEMALE	Total
	1 FAVOR	233	211	444
	2 OPPOSE	77	138	215
Total		310	349	659

Phi can be obtained in CROSSTABS by selecting it as a statistic.

Remember that Phi applies with 2 x 2 tables.

Symmetric Measures

		Value	Approx. Sig.
Nominal by Nominal	Phi	.157	.000
	Cramer's V	.157	.000
N of Valid Cases		659	

a. Not assuming the null hypothesis.

b. Using the asymptotic standard error assuming the null hypothesis.

The obtained result shows a phi coefficient of .157 which is significant at the .000 level. We would present this information as:

$$\phi = .16, \ p < .05$$

Using the same benchmark that we do with other correlations, we interpret this phi coefficient as an indication of a weak correlation between attitudes toward the death penalty and sex. Males are somewhat more likely than females to favor the death penalty for murder.

TABLES LARGER THAN 2 x 2 WITH NOMINAL DATA

The contingency coefficient and Cramér's V are two commonly used measures of correlation for tables with nominal level measures that are larger than 2 x 2. Both are derivatives or chi-square. Both are easily calculated and interpreted in a similar manner.

The contingency coefficient, however, has the important disadvantage that the number of rows and columns will influence the maximum size that it will take. That is, the contingency coefficient will not always vary between 0 and 1 (although it won't get bigger than 1). This happens in non-square tables (for example, 3 x 4, 5 x 3, etc.). The Cramér's V statistic does not depend on the size of the table and allows us to estimate the correlation between nominal level variables.

Both statistics may be obtained by checking their box in the CROSSTABS procedure.

For example, the GSS measures attitudes toward the courts by asking respondents whether they believe the court's dealing with criminals are too harsh (1), not harsh enough (2), or about right (3). We can look to see whether this varies by marital status: married (1), divorced (2), separated (3), widowed (4) and never married (5). Both variables are nominal. We have a 3 x 5 table which is suitable for the contingency coefficient and Cramér's V.

199

To obtain these statistics:

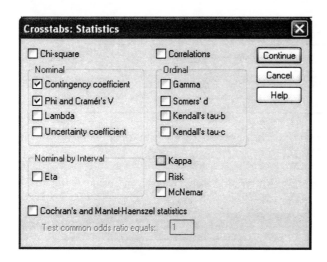

The computer output shows:

Symmetric Measures

		Value	Approx. Sig.
Nominal by Nominal	Phi	.159	.034
	Cramer's V	.112	.034
	Contingency Coefficient	.157	.034
N of Valid Cases		658	

a. Not assuming the null hypothesis.

b. Using the asymptotic standard error assuming the null hypothesis.

The Cramér's V shows that there is a weak correlation between attitudes toward the courts and marital status. V=.11, p<.05. The contingency coefficient also shows that there is a weak association between these variables. C=.157, p<.05.

SUMMARY

This chapter has examined non-parametric measures of correlation. Spearman's r and Goodman and Kruskal's Gamma are commonly used with ordinal level variables. Phi, the contingency coefficient and Cramér's V are used with nominal level variables with the choice of statistic depending on the size of the table.

As in all summary interpretations, you should strive to report:

- source of information
- the assumptions you've made to select a statistic
- the strength of the nonparametric statistic

KEY TERMS

Contingency coefficient
Cramér's V
Gamma
Nonparametric
Phi
Spearman's rank order correlation

Name _____   **Date** _____

1.   *Research Problems:* Use the General Social Survey to calculate Spearman's *r* to test the following hypotheses:

Research hypothesis 1.   Respondent's highest degree (DEGREE) is related to their mother's highest degree (MADEG).

Research hypothesis 2.   Add a pair of variables of your own selection.

Use the codebook to identify the characteristics of variables.

Record the correlation matrix for these variables (Spearman's *r)*.

Interpret the results

Name _____   **Date** _____

2.   *Research Problems:* Use the Monitoring the Future Survey to calculate Gamma to test the following hypotheses:

Research hypothesis 1.   Lifetime marijuana use (V115) is correlated with traffic tickets (V197).

Use the codebook to identify the characteristics of variables.

Record the Gamma statistic for these variables (G*)*.

Interpret the results

3.   Use Fox's Statistics Calculator to calculate Spearman's r.

A researcher was interested in determining whether class standing is related to time spent on-line on the Internet. He asked student to report how many hours they were on-line during the past week and correlated this with their grade on the exam. Grades are measured as (A+=9, A=8, B+=7, B=6,C+=5, C=4, D+=3, D=2, F=1). The information is:

Student	Time on internet (x)	Grade on test (y)
A	7	9
B	4	7
C	5	8
D	3	6
E	3	5
F	2	4
G	7	8
H	1	6

a.   What is Spearman's r? _____

b.   What is the critical value of r, assuming a value of .01? _____

c.   What is the critical value of r, assuming a value of .05? _____

d.   Is the correlation between grades and time on the internet significant at the .01 level?

e.   Is it significant at the .05 level?

f.   If appropriate, interpret the form, extent, and precision.

Name _____   **Date** _____

4.   *Research Problems:* Use the General Social Survey to calculate Cramer's V to test the
         following hypotheses:

Research hypothesis 1.   Attitudes toward abortion for any reason (ABANY) is correlated
                                with marital status (Marital).

Use the codebook to identify the characteristics of variables.

Record the Cramér's V statistic for these variables (V).

Interpret the results

Name _____   **Date** _____

5.   *Research Problems:* Use the General Social Survey or the Monitoring the Future Study to calculate Cramer's V for two variables of your choice:

Your hypothesis.

Use the codebook to identify the characteristics of variables.

Record the Cramér's V statistic for these variables (V*)*.

Interpret the results

INSTRUCTIONAL CODEBOOK

**SELECTED VARIABLES
FROM**

MONITORING THE FUTURE:
A CONTINUING STUDY OF AMERICAN YOUTH
(12TH – GRADE SURVEY), 2004

(ICPSR 4264)

Principal Investigators

Lloyd D. Johnston, Jerald G. Bachman,
Patrick M. O'Malley, and John E. Schulenberg

PREFACE

The following collection of data is a subset from the 2005 release of the longitudinal study of the lifestyles and values of youth in America. This codebook draws selected excerpts directly from the original study.

The data (and tabulations) utilized in this booklet were made available (in part) by the Inter-university Consortium for Political and Social Research (ICPSR). The data for MONITORING THE FUTURE: A CONTINUING STUDY OF AMERICAN YOUTH, Annual were originally collected by Lloyd D. Johnston, Jerald G. Bachman, Patrick M. O'Malley, and John E. Schulenberg. Neither the collector of the original data nor the Consortium bears any responsibility for the analyses or interpretations presented here.

DATA COLLECTION DESCRIPTION

MONITORING THE FUTURE: A CONTINUING STUDY OF THE LIFESTYLES AND VALUES OF YOUTH, Annual, which is conducted by the University of Michigan's Institute for Social Research and receives its core funding from the National Institute on Drug Abuse, is an unusually comprehensive research project in several respects: surveys are conducted annually on an ongoing basis; the samples are large and nationally representative; and the subject matter is very broad, encompassing some 1300 variables per year.

The Monitoring the Future Project is designed to explore changes in many important values, behaviors, and lifestyle orientations of contemporary American youth. Two general types of tasks may be distinguished. The first is to provide a systematic and accurate description of the youth population of interest in a given year, and to quantify the direction and rate of the changes taking place among them over time. The second task, more analytic than descriptive, involves the explanation of the relationships and trends observed to exist.

INTRODUCTION

DATA COLLECTION PROCEDURES

The basic research design involves annual data collections from high school seniors during the spring of each year, beginning with the class of 1975. Each data collection takes place in approximately 125 public and private high schools selected to provide an accurate cross-section of high school seniors throughout the United States.

One limitation in the design is that it does not include in the target population those young men and women who drop out of high school before graduation (or before the last few months of the senior year, to be more precise). This excludes a relatively small proportion of each age cohort -- between 15 and 20 percent -- though not an unimportant segment, since certain behaviors, such as drug usage and delinquency tend to be higher than average in this group. For the purposes of estimating changes from one cohort of high school seniors to another, the omission of dropouts represents a problem only if different cohorts have considerably different proportions who drop out. There is no reason to expect dramatic changes in those rates for the foreseeable future, and recently published government statistics indicate a great deal of stability in dropout rates since 1970.

CONTENT AREAS AND QUESTIONNAIRE DESIGN

Drug use and related attitudes are the topics which receive the most extensive coverage in the Monitoring the Future project; but the questionnaires also deal with a wide range of other subject areas, including attitudes about government, social institutions, race relations, changing roles for women, educational aspirations, occupational aims, and marital and family plans, as well as a variety of background and demographic factors.

FILE STRUCTURE

The variables described in this codebook are a subset taken from the core and form 1 of MONITORING THE FUTURE: A CONTINUING STUDY OF THE LIFESTYLES AND VALUES OF YOUTH, 2004. A full description of the original data structure, files, and representative publications can be obtained from the ICPSR data library.

The dataset is readable by the Statistical Package for the Social Sciences (SPSS © for Windows).

The instructional file is prepared for the SPSS 14.0 Student version which is limited to 50 variables and 1500 cases. A questions come from the core data set and form 1. A random sample of 1500 was drawn from the 2521 cases in the original file.

The instruction file has 49 variables and 1500 cases. It is named:

MTF 2004.sav

MISSING DATA

The original data file contained several missing codes for non-response. People may refuse to answer some questions, they don't know, or a question may have been not applicable. These codes are collapsed into a single category in the instructional dataset (usually as –9).

CODEBOOK INFORMATION

The codebook available for this study is not of the usual sort created by ICPSR. Rather, it is an edited version of the annual ISR volumes put into codebook form. It should also be noted that the codebook unlike the usual codebook is arranged by question numbers which do not coincide with the variable numbers. For user convenience, a sequential reference number has been added.

The example below is a reproduction of information appearing in the on-line codebook for a typical variable.

V139[1] **#X 'H'/LIFETIME**[2]   **REF 371**[3]
On how many occasions (if any) have you used heroin   (smack, horse, skag)... in your lifetime?[4]

1[5]	0 occasions[6]
2	1-2
3	3-5
4	6-9
5	10-19
6	20-39
7	40 or more

[1]   Mneumonic name of variable.
[2]   Variable label
[3]   Variable reference number
[4]   Text from the questionnaire giving the wording for the question.
[5]   Values in the data for the variable
[6]   Value label

VARIABLE DESCRIPTION LIST: INSTRUCTIONAL DATASET

VAR NO.	VARIABLE LABEL	REF NO.
V13	SCHL RGN-4 CAT	REF 1

School region
1. NORTHEAST: Maine, New Hampshire, Vermont, Massachusetts, Rhode Island, Connecticut, New York, New Jersey, and Pennsylvania
2. NORTH CENTRAL: Ohio, Indiana, Illinois, Michigan, Wisconsin, Minnesota, Iowa, Missouri, North Dakota, South Dakota, Nebraska, and Kansas
3. SOUTH: Delaware, Maryland, District of Columbia, Virginia, West Virginia, North Carolina, South Carolina, Georgia, Florida, Kentucky, Tennessee, Alabama Mississippi, Arkansas, Louisiana, Oklahoma, and Texas
4. WEST: Montana, Idaho, Wyoming, Colorado, New Mexico, Arizona, Utah, Nevada, Washington, Oregon, and California

V150	032C03 :R'S SEX	REF 2
	MISSING -9	

C03: What is your sex?
1. Male
2. Female

V151	032C04 :R'S RACE	REF 3
	MISSING -9	

C04: How do you describe yourself?
0. White or Caucasian
1. Black or Afro-American
NOTE: American Indian, Mexican American or Chicano, Puerto Rican or other Latin American, Oriental or Asian American, and Other were recoded to missing by the PI for reasons of confidentiality.

V49   # SIBLINGS   REF 4
          MISSING -9

C07ab: How many brothers and sisters do you have? (Include
step brothers and sisters and half-brothers and sisters.)
    0. None
    1. One
    2. Two
    3. Three or more

V163   032C08 :FATHR EDUC LEVEL   REF 5
          MISSING -9

C08: What is the highest level of schooling your father completed?
    1. Completed grade school or less
    2. Some high school
    3. Completed high school
    4. Some college
    5. Completed college
    6. Graduate or professional school after college

V164   032C09 :MOTHR EDUC LEVEL   REF 6
          MISSING -9

C09: What is the highest level of schooling your mother completed?
    1. Completed grade school or less
    2. Some high school
    3. Completed high school
    4. Some college
    5. Completed college
    6. Graduate or professional school after college

V166   032C11 :R'S POLTL PRFNC   REF 7
          MISSING -9, 5 through 8
C11: How would you describe your political preference?
    1. Strongly Republican
    2. Mildly Republican
    3. Mildly Democrat
    4. Strongly Democrat
    5. Independent Party
    6. No Preference
    7. Other

8. Don't know / Haven't decided

V167   **032C12 :R'POL BLF RADCL**   **REF 8**
      MISSING -9, 8
C12: How would you describe your political beliefs?
  1. Very conservative
  2. Conservative
  3. Moderate
  4. Liberal
  5. Very liberal
  6. Radical
  8. None of above/ Don't know

V176   **032C18B:#DA/4W SC MS CUT**   **REF 9**
      MISSING -9
C18: During the LAST FOUR WEEKS, how many whole days of school have you missed...

C18b: Because you skipped or "cut"
  1. None
  2. 1 day
  3. 2 days
  4. 3 days
  5. 4-5 days
  6. 6-10 days
  7. 11 or more

V179   **032C20 :R HS GRADE/D=1**   **REF 10**
      MISSING -9
C20: Which of the following best describes your average grade so far in high school?
  9. A (93-100)
  8. A- (90-92)
  7. B+ (87-89)
  6. B (83-86)
  5. B- (80-82)
  4. C+ (77-79)
  3. C (73-76)
  2. C- (70-72)
  1. D (69 or below)

V181   032C21B:R WL DO ARMD FC   **REF 11**
   MISSING -9

C21: How likely is it that you will do each of the following things after high school?
C21b: Serve in the armed forces
   1. Definitely won't
   2. Probably won't
   3. Probably will
   4. Definitely will

V183   032C21D:R WL DO 4YR CLG   **REF 12**
   MISSING -9

<See Q. C21 for complete question text.>
C21d: Graduate from 4-year college
   1. Definitely won't
   2. Probably won't
   3. Probably will
   4. Definitely will

V191   032C23 :HRS/W WRK SCHYR   **REF 13**
   MISSING -9

C23: On the average over the school year, how many hours per week do you work in a paid or unpaid job?
   1. None
   2. 5 or less hours
   3. 6 to 10 hours
   4. 11 to 15 hours
   5. 16 to 20 hours
   6. 21 to 25 hours
   7. 26 to 30 hours
   8. More than 30 hours

V192   032C24A:R$/AVG WEEK JOB   **REF 14**
   MISSING -9

C24: During an average week, how much money do you get from...
C24a: A job or other work
   1. None
   2. $1-5
   3. $6-10
   4. $11-20
   5. $21-35
   6. $36-50
   7. $51-75

8. $76-125
9. $126+

V194   032C25 :#X/AV WK GO OUT   REF 15
MISSING -9
C25: During a typical week, on how many evenings do you go out for fun and recreation?
   1. Less than one
   2. One
   3. Two
   4. Three
   5. Four or five
   6. Six or seven

V196   032C27 :DRIVE>200 MI/WK   REF 16
MISSING -9
C27: During an average week, how much do you usually drive a car, truck, or motorcycle?
   1. Not at all
   2. 1 to 10 miles
   3. 11 to 50 miles
   4. 51 to 100 miles
   5. 100 to 200 miles
   6. More than 200 miles

V197   032C28 :#X/12MO R TCKTD   REF 17
MISSING -9
C28: Within the LAST 12 MONTHS, how many times, if any, have you received a ticket (OR been stopped and warned) for moving violations, such as speeding, running a stop light, or improper passing?
   0. None--GO TO Q. C30
   1. Once
   2. Twice
   3. Three times
   4. Four or more times

V101   032B01 :EVR SMK CIG,REGL   REF 18
MISSING -9
B01: Have you ever smoked cigarettes?
   1. Never--Go to Question B03
   2. Once or twice
   3. Occasionally but not regularly
   4. Regularly in the past

5. Regularly now

V103   032B03 :EVER DRINK   REF 19
        MISSING -9

B03: Next we want to ask you about drinking alcoholic beverages, including beer, wine, wine coolers, and liquor.

Have you ever had any beer, wine, wine coolers, or liquor to drink?
    1. No--Go to Q. B07
    2. Yes

V104   032B04A:#X DRNK/LIFETIME   REF 20
        MISSING -9

B04: On how many occasions have you had alcoholic beverages to drink...

B04a: Alcohol in your lifetime?
    1. 0 occasions (includes 1. in B03)
    2. 1-2
    3. 3-5
    4. 6-9
    5. 10-19
    6. 20-39
    7. 40 or more

V106   032B04C:#X DRNK/LAST30DA   REF 21
        MISSING -9

<See Q. B04 for complete question text.>
B04c: Alcohol during the last 30 days?
    1. 0 occasions (includes 1. in B03)
    2. 1-2
    3. 3-5
    4. 6-9
    5. 10-19
    6. 20-39
    7. 40 or more

V108   032B06 :5+DRK ROW/LST 2W   REF 22
        MISSING -9

B06: Think back over the LAST TWO WEEKS. How many times have you had five or more drinks in a row? (A "drink" is a bottle of beer, a glass of wine, a wine cooler, a shot glass of liquor, or a mixed drink.)

1. None (includes 1. in B03)
2. Once
3. Twice
4. Three to five times
5. Six to nine times
6. Ten or more times

THE NEXT MAJOR SECTION OF THIS QUESTIONNAIRE DEALS WITH VARIOUS OTHER DRUGS. THERE IS A LOT OF TALK THESE DAYS ABOUT THIS SUBJECT, BUT VERY LITTLE ACCURATE INFORMATION.

THEREFORE, WE STILL HAVE A LOT TO LEARN ABOUT THE ACTUAL EXPERIENCES AND ATTITUDES OF PEOPLE YOUR AGE.

WE HOPE THAT YOU CAN ANSWER ALL QUESTIONS; BUT IF YOU FIND ONE WHICH YOU FEEL YOU CANNOT ANSWER HONESTLY, WE WOULD PREFER THAT YOU LEAVE IT BLANK.

REMEMBER THAT YOUR ANSWERS WILL BE KEPT STRICTLY CONFIDENTIAL: THEY ARE NEVER CONNECTED WITH YOUR NAME OR YOUR CLASS.

V115   032B07A:#XMJ+HS/LIFETIME   REF 23
          MISSING -9
B07: On how many occasions (if any) have you used marijuana (grass, pot) or hashish (hash, hash oil)...

B07a: Marijuana/hashish in your lifetime?
1. 0 occasions
2. 1-2
3. 3-5
4. 6-9
5. 10-19
6. 20-39
7. 40 or more

V117   032B07C:#XMJ+HS/LAST30DA   REF 24
          MISSING -9
\<See Q. B07 for complete question text.\>
B07c: Marijuana/hashish during the last 30 days?

1. 0 occasions

   2. 1-2
   3. 3-5
   4. 6-9
   5. 10-19
   6. 20-39
   7. 40 or more

V124   032B10A:#X COKE/LIFETIME   REF 25
      MISSING -9
B10: On how many occasions (if any) have you used cocaine...
B10a: Cocaine in your lifetime?

   1. 0 occasions
   2. 1-2
   3. 3-5
   4. 6-9
   5. 10-19
   6. 20-39
   7. 40 or more

V126   032B10C:#X COKE/LAST30DA   REF 26
      MISSING -9
<See Q. B10 for complete question text.>
B10c: Cocaine during the last 30 days?
   1. 0 occasions
   2. 1-2
   3. 3-5
   4. 6-9
   5. 10-19
   6. 20-39
   7. 40 or more

V139   032B15A:#X 'H'/LIFETIME   REF 27
      MISSING -9
B15: On how many occasions (if any) have you used heroin (smack, horse, skag)...
B15a: Heroin in your lifetime?
   1. 0 occasions
   2. 1-2
   3. 3-5
   4. 6-9
   5. 10-19
   6. 20-39

7. 40 or more

V141   **032B15C:#X 'H'/LAST 30DA**   **REF 28**
      MISSING -9
<See Q. B15 for complete question text.>
B15c: Heroin during the last 30 days?
    1. 0 occasions
    2. 1-2
    3. 3-5
    4. 6-9
    5. 10-19
    6. 20-39
    7. 40 or more

V1643   **031A006C:SAT PRSNL SAFTY**   **REF 29**
      MISSING -9
    A06: How satisfied are you with...
<See Q. A06 for complete question text.>
    A06c: Your personal safety in your neighborhood, on your job, and in your school—safety
from being attacked and injured in some way?
    7. Completely satisfied
    6. .
    5. .
    4. Neutral
    3. .
    2. .
    1. Completely dissatisfied

V1646   **031A006F:SAT OWN FRIENDS**   **REF 30**
      MISSING -9
<See Q. A06 for complete question text.>
A06f: Your friends and other people you spend time with?
    7. Completely satisfied
    6. .
    5. .
    4. Neutral
    3. .
    2. .
    1. Completely dissatisfied

V1647   **031A006G:SAT GT ALNG PRN**   **REF 31**

MISSING -9
<See Q. A06 for complete question text.>
A06g: The way you get along with your parents?
   7. Completely satisfied
   6. .
   5. .
   4. Neutral
   3. .
   2. .
   1. Completely dissatisfied

V1652   031A006L:SAT LIFE AS WHL   REF 32
MISSING -9
<See Q. A06 for complete question text.>
A06l: Your life as a whole these days?
   7. Completely satisfied
   6. .
   5. .
   4. Neutral
   3. .
   2. .
   1. Completely dissatisfied

V1653   031A006M:SAT GOVT OPRTNG   REF 33
MISSING -9
<See Q. A06 for complete question text.>
A06m: The way our national government is operating?'

   7. Completely satisfied
   6. .
   5. .
   4. Neutral
   3. .
   2. .
   1. Completely dissatisfied

V1672   031A011A:-OBY LW=-GD CTZ   REF 34
MISSING -9

A11: These next questions ask your opinions about a number of different topics. How much do you agree or disagree with each statement below?

A11a: I feel that you can't be a good citizen unless you always obey the law
1. Disagree
2. Mostly disagree
3. Neither
4. Mostly agree
5. Agree

V1673   031A011B:GD CTZN ALG GOV   REF 35
MISSING -9
<See Q. A11 for complete question text.>
A11b: I feel a good citizen should go along with whatever the government does even if he disagrees with it
1. Disagree
2. Mostly disagree
3. Neither
4. Mostly agree
5. Agree

V1674   031A011C:GD CTZN CHG GOV   REF 36
MISSING -9
<See Q. A11 for complete question text.>
A11c: I feel a good citizen tries to change the government policies he disagrees with
1. Disagree
2. Mostly disagree
3. Neither
4. Mostly agree
5. Agree

V1766   031A012A:RSK OF CIG1+PK/   REF 37
MISSING -9
A12: The next questions ask for your opinions on the effects of using certain drugs and other substances. How much do you think people risk harming themselves (physically or in other ways), if they...

A12a: Smoke one or more packs of cigarettes per day
1. No risk
2. Slight risk
3. Moderate risk
4. Great risk

V1767   031A012B:RSK OF MJ 1-2 X   REF 38
MISSING -9

<See Q. A12 for complete question text.>
A12b: Try marijuana once or twice
   1. No risk
   2. Slight risk
   3. Moderate risk
   4. Great risk

V1770   **031A012E:RSK COK PWDR 1-**   **REF 39**
       MISSING -9
<See Q. A12 for complete question text.>
A12e: Try cocaine in powder form once or twice
   1. No risk
   2. Slight risk
   3. Moderate risk
   4. Great risk

V1773   **031A012H:RSK CRACK 1-2X**   **REF 40**
       MISSING -9
<See Q. A12 for complete question text.>
A12h: Try "crack" cocaine once or twice
   1. No risk
   2. Slight risk
   3. Moderate risk
   4. Great risk

V1776   **031A012K:RSK OF 1-2 DRIN**   **REF 41**
       MISSING -9
<See Q. A12 for complete question text.>
A12k: Try one or two drinks of an alcoholic beverage (beer, wine, liquor)
   1. No risk
   2. Slight risk
   3. Moderate risk
   4. Great risk

V1779   **031A012N:RSK OF 5+DR/WKN**   **REF 42**
       MISSING -9
<See Q. A12 for complete question text.>
A12n: Have five or more drinks once or twice each weekend
   1. No risk
   2. Slight risk
   3. Moderate risk

4. Great risk

V1780   031A013A:EASY GT MARIJUA   REF 43
        MISSING -9
    A13: How difficult do you think it would be for you to get each of the following types of drugs, if you wanted some?

    A13a: Marijuana
        1. Probably impossible
        2. Very difficult
        3. Fairly difficult
        4. Fairly easy
        5. Very easy

VAR 1781   031A013B:EASY GT CRACK   REF 44
        MISSING -9
    <See Q. A13 for complete question text.>
    A13b: "Crack" cocaine
        1. Probably impossible
        2. Very difficult
        3. Fairly difficult
        4. Fairly easy
        5. Very easy

V1782   031A013C:EASY GT COK PWD   REF 45
        MISSING -9
    <See Q. A13 for complete question text.>
    A13c: Cocaine powder
        1. Probably impossible
        2. Very difficult
        3. Fairly difficult
        4. Fairly easy
        5. Very easy
THE NEXT QUESTIONS ARE ABOUT YOUR EXPERIENCES IN SCHOOL.

V1682   031D001 :R LIKES SCHOOL   REF 46
        MISSING -9
    D01: Some people like school very much. Others don't. How do you feel about going to school?
        5. I like school very much
        4. I like school quite a lot

3. I like school some
2. I don't like school very much
1. I don't like school at all

V1687   031D006 :STDTS DSLK CHTG   REF 47
MISSING -9

D06: How do you think most of the students in your classes would feel if you cheated on a test?

1. They would like it very much
2. They would like it
3. They would not care
4. They would dislike it
5. They would dislike it very much

V1733   031D016A:#X/12M DOC-CHEK   REF 48
MISSING -9

D16: In the LAST 12 MONTHS, how many times (if any) have you seen a doctor or other professional for each of the following

D16a: For a routine physical check-up

1. None
2. Once
3. Twice
4. 3 to 5 times
5. 6 to 9 times
6. 10+ times

V1734   031D016B:#X/12M DOC-FGHT   REF 49
MISSING -9

<See Q. D16 for complete question text.>
D16b: For an injury suffered in a fight, assault, or auto accident

1. None
2. Once
3. Twice
4. 3 to 5 times
5. 6 to 9 times
6. 10+ times

INDEX OF VARIABLE NUMBERS TO REFERENCE NUMBERS

The variable numbers in the dataset are not listed sequentially since they may come from the core or form one (one of the six forms) of the questionnaire. This list gives the variable numbers cross-listed against their reference numbers. The reference numbers are sequential for this codebook.

V13	SCHL RGN-4 CAT	REF 1
V49	# SIBLINGS	REF 4
V101	032B01 :EVR SMK CIG,REGL	REF 18
V103	032B03 :EVER DRINK	REF 19
V104	032B04A:#X DRNK/LIFETIME	REF 20
V106	032B04C:#X DRNK/LAST30DA	REF 21
V108	032B06 :5+DRK ROW/LST 2W	REF 22
V115	032B07A:#XMJ+HS/LIFETIME	REF 23
V117	032B07C:#XMJ+HS/LAST30DA	REF 24
V124	032B10A:#X COKE/LIFETIME	REF 25
V126	032B10C:#X COKE/LAST30DA	REF 26
V139	032B15A:#X 'H'/LIFETIME	REF 27
V141	032B15C:#X 'H'/LAST 30DA	REF 28
V150	032C03 :R'S SEX	REF 2
V151	032C04 :R'S RACE	REF 3
V163	032C08 :FATHR EDUC LEVEL	REF 5
V164	032C09 :MOTHR EDUC LEVEL	REF 6
V166	032C11 :R'S POLTL PRFNC	REF 7
V167	032C12 :R'POL BLF RADCL	REF 8
V176	032C18B:#DA/4W SC MS CUT	REF 9
V179	032C20 :R HS GRADE/D=1	REF 10
V181	032C21B:R WL DO ARMD FC	REF 11
V183	032C21D:R WL DO 4YR CLG	REF 12
V191	032C23 :HRS/W WRK SCHYR	REF 13
V192	032C24A:R$/AVG WEEK JOB	REF 14
V194	032C25 :#X/AV WK GO OUT	REF 15
V196	032C27 :DRIVE>200 MI/WK	REF 16
V197	032C28 :#X/12MO R TCKTD	REF 17
V1643	031A006C:SAT PRSNL SAFTY	REF 29
V1646	031A006F:SAT OWN FRIENDS	REF 30
V1647	031A006G:SAT GT ALNG PRN	REF 31
V1652	031A006L:SAT LIFE AS WHL	REF 32
V1653	031A006M:SAT GOVT OPRTNG	REF 33
V1672	031A011A:-OBY LW=-GD CTZ	REF 34
V1673	031A011B:GD CTZN ALG GOV	REF 35

V1674	031A011C:GD CTZN CHG GOV	REF 36
V1682	031D001 :R LIKES SCHOOL	REF 46
V1687	031D006 :STDTS DSLK CHTG	REF 47
V1733	031D016A:#X/12M DOC-CHEK	REF 48
V1734	031D016B:#X/12M DOC-FGHT	REF 49
V1766	031A012A:RSK OF CIG1+PK/	REF 37
V1767	031A012B:RSK OF MJ 1-2 X	REF 38
V1770	031A012E:RSK COK PWDR 1-	REF 39
V1773	031A012H:RSK CRACK 1-2X	REF 40
V1776	031A012K:RSK OF 1-2 DRIN	REF 41
V1779	031A012N:RSK OF 5+DR/WKN	REF 42
V1780	031A013A:EASY GT MARIJUA	REF 43
V1781	031A013B:EASY GT CRACK	REF 44
V1782	031A013C:EASY GT COK PWD	REF 45

INSTRUCTIONAL CODEBOOK

SELECTED VARIABLES
FROM

GENERAL SOCIAL SURVEY, 2004

Principal Investigators

James A. Davis, Tom W. Smith
and Peter V. Marsden

PREFACE

The following collection of data is a subset from the 2004 release of the General Social Survey (GSS) in the United States. This codebook draws selected excerpts directly from the original study. The cumulative codebook for the GSS should be consulted for the exact wording of questions.

The data (and tabulations) utilized in this booklet were made available (in part) by the Inter-university Consortium for Political and Social Research (ICPSR). The data for the GENERAL SOCIAL SURVEY, 1972-2004 were originally collected by the National Opinion Research Center (NORC). Neither the collector of the original data nor the Consortium bears any responsibility for the analyses or interpretations presented here.

DATA COLLECTION DESCRIPTION

The GENERAL SOCIAL SURVEY, 2004 which is conducted by NORC is the definitive study of public opinion in the United States. The GSS is conducted every second year. The 2004 GSS uses a double sample method (twice the size of the previous annual GSS surveys) with eight topic modules. This instructional dataset draws from the 2004 survey. The surveys are conducted bi-annually on an ongoing basis; the samples are large and nationally representative; and the subject matter is very broad, encompassing about 1000 variables per year.

The GSS is designed to explore trends in public opinion in the USA and to allow international research using two International Social Survey Program modules.

DATA COLLECTION PROCEDURES

The basic research design involves annual in-person data collections from adults. A multi-stage probability sample based on regional status and metropolitan areas, county size, and housing units is used to select respondents. The full survey includes several weighting variables to account for sampling. The instructional dataset does not use these weights. The cumulative codebook provides an extensive discussion of sampling procedures. The study is designed to be representative of the adult population in the USA.

CONTENT AREAS AND QUESTIONNAIRE DESIGN

The GSS is perhaps the most extensive collection of data on public opinion in America. Extensive research has been done on pretty much any social science topic you can name, and on how to best ask a question about the topic.

GSS WEBSITE

　　　　The National Opinion Research Center and ICPSR have developed an on-line codebook for the General Social Survey. The data for this workbook was extracted from this website and converted into an SPSS data file.

　　　　You will need to access this web-site to obtain the exact wording of some of the questions from the GSS. The codebook in this appendix provides a summary description of variables. The web-site for the cumulative codebook is shown below.

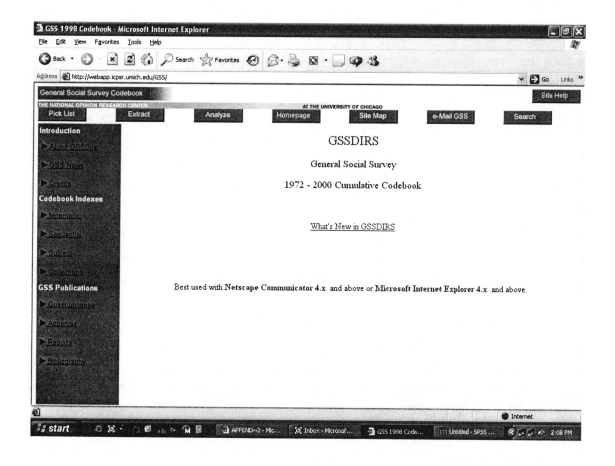

　　　　There are several methods that you can use to obtain codebook information from this site. In many instances you will simply be looking for information about a few variables. Click on the link to the Mneumonic index (on the left side of the screen) to go to an alphabetical list of mneumonic variable names.

　　　　I choose to pull up information about abortion for ABANY. The codebook provides the exact question wording, the question number(s) on the survey, and some information about frequency distributions by year of the survey.

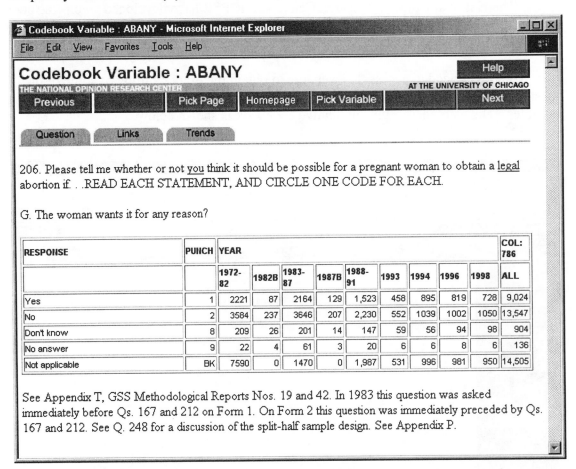

The table above shows annual frequencies for 1993, 1994, 1996, and 1998. Other years are grouped to simplify the presentation of the table. You may get the information for each individual year by using the cumulative file. This can easily be done on-line by clicking on ANALYZE on the GSS homepage.

FILE STRUCTURE

The variables described in this codebook are a subset of 49 variables from GSS 2004. They were extracted using the GSS web-site by clicking on ANALYZE and using the survey documentation and extraction functions. A full description of the original data structure, files, and representative publications can be obtained from the web-site.

http://webapp.icpsr.umich.edu/GSS

The dataset is readable by the Statistical Package for the Social Sciences (SPSS © for Windows). A random sample of 1500 of 2812 cases was selected so that the data set could be analyzed using SPSS Student Version.

The instructional SPSS file is named: GSS 2004.sav

MISSING DATA

The original data file contained several missing codes for non-response. People may refuse to answer some questions, they don't know, or a question may have been not applicable. These codes are identified as "M" in the instructional codebook.

CODEBOOK INFORMATION

The codebook available for this study was generated as an SPSS Data Dictionary using the variable and value labels provided by ICPSR in the data extraction. The questions on abortion, policing, and suicide were edited to improve the meaningfulness of the codebook for these variables. The labeling of other variables is generally clear. If you are not certain, please consult the GSS Cumulative codebook. Note that the variable names in this appendix are arranged in alphabetical order based on variable mneumonics.

File Type: SPSS Data File   gss 2004.sav

Total # of Defined Variable Elements: 49
Data Are Not Weighted

Variable names are in **BOLD**

Please tell me whether or not <u>you</u> think it should be possible for a pregnant woman to obtain a <u>legal</u> abortion if. . .READ EACH STATEMENT, AND CIRCLE ONE CODE FOR EACH.

ABANY   The woman wants it for any reason?
     Missing Values: 0, 8, 9
     Value   Label
       0 M NAP
       1   YES
       2   NO
       8 M DK
       9 M NA

ABRAPE   If she becomes pregnant as a result of rape?
    Missing Values: 0, 8, 9
    Value   Label
      0 M NAP
      1   YES
      2   NO
      8 M DK
      9 M NA

ABSINGLE If she is not married and does not want to marry the man?

    Missing Values: 0, 8, 9
    Value   Label
      0 M NAP
      1   YES
      2   NO
      8 M DK
      9 M NA

AGE   Age of respondent
    Missing Values: 99
    Value   Label
      98   DK
      99 M NA

CAPPUN   Favor or oppose death penalty for murder
    Missing Values: 0, 8, 9
    Value   Label
      0 M NAP
      1   FAVOR
      2   OPPOSE
      8 M DK
      9 M NA

CLASS   Subjective class identification
    Missing Values: 8, 9
    Value   Label
      1   LOWER CLASS
      2   WORKING CLASS
      3   MIDDLE CLASS
      4   UPPER CLASS
      5   NO CLASS

8 M DK
9 M NA

CONDOM   Used condom last time
Missing Values: 8, 9
Value   Label
1   Yes used condom
2   not used condom
8 M DK
9 M NA

COURTS   Courts dealing with criminals
Missing Values: 0, 8, 9
Value   Label
0 M NAP
1   Too harsh
2   Not harsh enough
3   About right
8 M DK
9 M NA

DEGREE   Respondent's highest degree
Missing Values: 7, 8, 9
Value   Label
0   LT HIGH SCHOOL
1   HIGH SCHOOL
2   JUNIOR COLLEGE
3   BACHELOR
4   GRADUATE
7 M NAP
8 M DK
9 M NA

FEAR   Afraid to walk at night in neighborhood
Missing Values: 0, 8, 9
Value   Label
0 M NAP
1   YES
2   NO
8 M DK
9 M NA

GRASS   Should marijuana be made legal
    Missing Values: 0, 8, 9
    Value   Label
      0 M NAP
      1   LEGAL
      2   NOT LEGAL
      8 M DK
      9 M NA

GUNLAW   Favor or oppose gun permits
    Missing Values: 0, 8, 9
    Value   Label
      0 M NAP
      1   FAVOR
      2   OPPOSE
      8 M DK
      9 M NA

HAPPY   General happiness
    Missing Values: 0, 8, 9
    Value   Label
      0 M NAP
      1   Very happy
      2   Pretty happy
      3   Not too happy
      8 M DK
      9 M NA

HEALTH   Condition of health
    Missing Values: 0, 8, 9
    Value   Label
      0 M NAP
      1   EXCELLENT
      2   GOOD
      3   FAIR
      4   POOR
      8 M DK
      9 M NA

HELPPOOR   Should government improve standard of living?
    Missing Values: 0, 8, 9
    Value   Label

0 M NAP
1   Government action
2
3 Agree with both
4
5 People help selves
8 M DK
9 M NA

HELPSICK   Should government help pay for medical care?
Missing Values: 0, 8, 9
Value   Label
0 M NAP
1   Government action
2
3 Agree with both
4
5 People help selves
8 M DK
9 M NA

HGUNLAW   Should be more restrictions on handguns?
Missing Values: 0, 8, 9
Value   Label
0 M NAP
1   Agree
2   Disagree
8 M DK
9 M NA

INCOME98 Total family income (standardized to 1998 dollars)
Missing Values: 24, 98, 99
Value   Label
1   UNDER $1 000
2   $1 000 to 2 999
3   $3 000 to 3 999
4   $4 000 to 4 999
5   $5 000 to 5 999
6   $6 000 to 6 999
7   $7 000 to 7 999
8   $8 000 to 9 999
9   $10000 to 12499

    10   $12500 to 14999
    11   $15000 to 17499
    12   $17500 to 19999
    13   $20000 to 22499
    14   $22500 to 24999
    15   $25000 to 29999
    16   $30000 to 34999
    17   $35000 to 39999
    18   $40000 to 49999
    19   $50000 to 59999
    20   $60000 to 74999
    21   $75000 to $89999
    22   $90000 - $109999
    23   $110000 or over
    24 M REFUSED
    98 M DK
    99 M NA

MADEG   Mothers highest degree
    Missing Values: 7, 8, 9
    Value   Label
        0   LT HIGH SCHOOL
        1   HIGH SCHOOL
        2   JUNIOR COLLEGE
        3   BACHELOR
        4   GRADUATE
        7 M NAP
        8 M DK
        9 M NA

MARITAL   Marital status
    Missing Values: 9
    Value   Label
        1   MARRIED
        2   WIDOWED
        3   DIVORCED
        4   SEPARATED
        5   NEVER MARRIED
        9 M NA

NEWS   How often does R read newspaper?
    Missing Values: 0, 8, 9

Value   Label
0 M NAP
1   EVERYDAY
2   FEW TIMES A WEEK
3   ONCE A WEEK
4   LESS THAN ONCE WK
5   NEVER
8 M DK
9 M NA

OWNGUN   Have gun in home
Missing Values: 3, 8, 9
Value   Label
1   YES
2   NO
3 M REFUSED
8 M DK
9 M NA

PADEG   Fathers highest degree
Missing Values: 7, 8, 9
Value   Label
0   LT HIGH SCHOOL
1   HIGH SCHOOL
2   JUNIOR COLLEGE
3   BACHELOR
4   GRADUATE
7 M NAP
8 M DK
9 M NA

PARTYID Political party affiliation
Missing Values: 7, 8, 9
Value   Label
0   STRONG DEMOCRAT
1   NOT STR DEMOCRAT
2   IND,NEAR DEM
3   INDEPENDENT
4   IND,NEAR REP
5   NOT STR REPUBLICAN
6   STRONG REPUBLICAN
7 M OTHER PARTY

       8 M DK
       9 M NA

Several questions about police:

Are there any situations you can imagine in which you would approve of a policeman striking an adult male citizen?

<u>IF YES OR NOT SURE</u>: Would you approve of a policeman striking a citizen who:

POLABUSE A. Had said vulgar and obscene things to the policeman?
    Missing Values: 0, 8, 9
    Value   Label
      0 M NAP
      1   YES
      2   NO
      8 M DK
      9 M NA

POLATTAK Was attacking the policeman with his fists?
    Missing Values: 0, 8, 9
    Value   Label
      0 M NAP
      1   YES
      2   NO
      8 M DK
      9 M NA

POLHITOK Are there any situations you can imagine in which you would approve of a policeman striking an adult male citizen?
    Missing Values: 0, 8, 9
    Value   Label
      0 M NAP
      1   YES
      2   NO
      8 M DK
      9 M NA

POLVIEWS Think of self as liberal or conservative
    Missing Values: 0, 8, 9
    Value   Label
      0 M NAP
      1   EXTREMELY LIBERAL
      2   LIBERAL

   3   SLIGHTLY LIBERAL
   4   MODERATE
   5   SLGHTLY CONSERVATIVE
   6   CONSERVATIVE
   7   EXTRMLY CONSERVATIVE
   8 M DK
   9 M NA

PORNLAW   Feelings about pornography laws
   Missing Values: 0, 8, 9
   Value   Label
   0 M NAP
   1   ILLEGAL TO ALL
   2   ILLEGAL UNDER 18
   3   LEGAL
   8 M DK
   9 M NA

PRAY   How often does R pray
   Missing Values: 0, 8, 9
   Value   Label
   0 M NAP
   1   SEVERAL TIMES A DAY
   2   ONCE A DAY
   3   SEVERAL TIMES A WEEK
   4   ONCE A WEEK
   5   LT ONCE A WEEK
   6   NEVER
   8 M DK
   9 M NA

PREMARSX SEX BEFORE MARRIAGE
   Missing Values: 0, 8, 9
   Value   Label
   0 M NAP
   1   ALWAYS WRONG
   2   ALMST ALWAYS WRG
   3   SOMETIMES WRONG
   4   NOT WRONG AT ALL
   5   OTHER
   8 M DK
   9 M NA

RACE   Race of respondent
>   Value   Label
>   1   White
>   2   Black
>   3   Other

REGION   Region of interview
>   Value   Label
>   0   NOT ASSIGNED
>   1   NEW ENGLAND
>   2   MIDDLE ATLANTIC
>   3   E. NOR. CENTRAL
>   4   W. NOR. CENTRAL
>   5   SOUTH ATLANTIC
>   6   E. SOU. CENTRAL
>   7   W. SOU. CENTRAL
>   8   MOUNTAIN
>   9   PACIFIC

RELIG   Rs religious preference
>   Missing Values: 0, 98, 99
>   Value   Label
>   0 M NAP
>   1   Protestant
>   2   Catholic
>   3   Jewish
>   4   None
>   5   OTHER (SPECIFY)
>   6   BUDDHISM
>   7   HINDUISM
>   8   OTHER EASTERN
>   9   MOSLEM/ISLAM
>   10   Orthodox-christian
>   11   Chrsitian
>   12   NATIVE AMERICAN
>   13   INTER-NONDENOMINATIONAL
>   98 M DK
>   99 M NA

RINCOM98 Respondent's income   (Standardized to 1998 dollars)
>   Missing Values: 24, 98, 99
>   Value   Label

1 UNDER $1 000
2 $1 000 to 2 999
3 $3 000 to 3 999
4 $4 000 to 4 999
5 $5 000 to 5 999
6 $6 000 to 6 999
7 $7 000 to 7 999
8 $8 000 to 9 999
9 $10000 to 12499
10 $12500 to 14999
11 $15000 to 17499
12 $17500 to 19999
13 $20000 to 22499
14 $22500 to 24999
15 $25000 to 29999
16 $30000 to 34999
17 $35000 to 39999
18 $40000 to 49999
19 $50000 to 59999
20 $60000 to 74999
21 $75000 - $89999
22 $90000- $109999
23 $110 000 over
24 M REFUSED
98 M DK
99 M NA

SATJOB Satisfaction with job or housework?
Missing Values: 0, 8, 9
Value Label
0 M NAP
1 Very satisfied
2 Moderately satisfied
3 A little dissatisfied
4 Very dissatisfied
8 M DK
9 M NA

SEI Respondent's socioeconomic index Range 17.0 to 97.2 with higher numbers indicating higher status.

Based on methods developed by Otis Dudley Duncan, Keiko Nakao and Judith Treas have calculated a new scale for socioeconomic status. This is based on their 1989 GSS study of occupational prestige (See GSS Methodological Report No. 74.)

SEX   Respondents sex
Value   Label
  1   MALE
  2   FEMALE

SEXEDUC   Sex education in public schools?
Missing Values: 0, 8, 9
Value   Label
  0 M NAP
  1   Favor
  2   Oppose
  8 M DK
  9 M NA

SEXFREQ   Frequency of sex during last year
Missing Values: 8, 9
Value   Label
  0   Not at all
  1   Once or twice
  2   About once/month
  3   2-3 times/month
  4   About once/week
  5   2-3 times a week
  6   4-more times/wk
  8 M DK
  9 M NA

SOCBAR   Spend evening at bar
Missing Values: -1, 8, 9
Value   Label
  1   ALMOST DAILY
  2   SEV TIMES A WEEK
  3   SEV TIMES A MNTH
  4   ONCE A MONTH
  5   SEV TIMES A YEAR
  6   ONCE A YEAR
  7   NEVER
  8 M DK

9 M NA
-1 M NAP

SOCFREND Spend evening with friends
Missing Values: -1, 8, 9
Value   Label
   1   ALMOST DAILY
   2   SEV TIMES A WEEK
   3   SEV TIMES A MNTH
   4   ONCE A MONTH
   5   SEV TIMES A YEAR
   6   ONCE A YEAR
   7   NEVER
   8 M DK
   9 M NA
   -1 M NAP

SOCOMMUN Spend evening with neighbor
Missing Values: -1, 8, 9
Value   Label
   1   ALMOST DAILY
   2   SEV TIMES A WEEK
   3   SEV TIMES A MNTH
   4   ONCE A MONTH
   5   SEV TIMES A YEAR
   6   ONCE A YEAR
   7   NEVER
   8 M DK
   9 M NA
   -1 M NAP

SOCREL   Spend evening with relatives
Missing Values: -1, 8, 9
Value   Label
   1   ALMOST DAILY
   2   SEV TIMES A WEEK
   3   SEV TIMES A MNTH
   4   ONCE A MONTH
   5   SEV TIMES A YEAR
   6   ONCE A YEAR
   7   NEVER
   8 M DK

9 M NA
-1 M NAP

Three (of original four) questions on suicide:

Do you think a person has the right to end his or her own life if this person . . .

SUICIDE1 ... has an incurable disease?
     Missing Values: 0, 8, 9
     Value   Label
      0 M NAP
      1   YES
      2   NO
      8 M DK
      9 M NA

SUICIDE2 ... has gone bankrupt?
     Missing Values: 0, 8, 9
     Value   Label
      0 M NAP
      1   YES
      2   NO
      8 M DK
      9 M NA

SUICIDE4 ... is tired of living and ready to die?
     Missing Values: 0, 8, 9
     Value   Label
      0 M NAP
      1   YES
      2   NO
      8 M DK
      9 M NA

TVHOURS Hours per day watching tv
     Missing Values: -1, 98, 99
     Value   Label
      98 M DK
      99 M NA
      -1 M NAP

XMARSEX Sex with person other than spouse

Missing Values: 0, 8, 9
Value   Label
  0 M NAP
  1   ALWAYS WRONG
  2   ALMST ALWAYS WRG
  3   SOMETIMES WRONG
  4   NOT WRONG AT ALL
  5   OTHER
  8 M DK
  9 M NA